# The Francis Feud

## Why and How Conservative Catholics Squabble about Pope Francis

### Karl Keating

RASSELAS
HOUSE

Published by Rasselas House
El Cajon, California
RasselasHouse.com

Cover photo from Shutterstock.com
Formatting by PolgarusStudio.com

ISBN 978-1-942596-30-1 Ebook
ISBN 978-1-942596-37-0 Paperback

# Contents

# Introduction

When is it proper to criticize a reigning pope? Is it ever—
or never—proper? Might it be sometimes proper, even if
not always proper? And is *proper* even the right word?
The term suggests something right or permissible but not
necessary or compelled. Perhaps the question should be:
when is it *necessary* to criticize a reigning pope? If there
are necessary times, who should do the criticizing—high-
level Churchmen, well-degreed academics, well-read
laymen—maybe even the Catholic next door who has a
gripe?

Those are some of the questions examined in the
following pages, which are organized around three recently-
published books that view Pope Francis critically: Henry
Sire's *The Dictator Pope*,[1] Philip F. Lawler's *Lost Shepherd*,[2]
and Ross Douthat's *To Change the Church*.[3] Their
arguments are presented and discussed partly in their own
words and partly in the words of their reviewers, supporters,
and opponents—and partly in my words because I have
been both an observer and a participant.

\* \* \*

*De mortuis nihil nisi bonum*: speak no ill of the dead. It's an old Latin phrase, made popular in the fifteenth century by a Camaldolese monk, Ambrose Traversari, who translated into Latin a line from Diogenes Laërtius (A.D. 300), who in turn was quoting Chilon of Sparta (600 B.C.). In other words, the saying has been around a long time. If you speak it aloud, in English, all heads nod, but people realize that the saying has a time limit. It's usually understood to mean "speak no ill of the recently dead." A funeral is a place to eulogize the dearly departed, not to enumerate his faults.

As time goes on, people begin to feel free to criticize the deceased, at least if he had been a person of note or notoriety, whether in politics, the arts, or some other field, including religion. This applies even to popes. No one will complain if you bring up something unflattering about a long-deceased pope. "Innocent X was feared by his servants." "Julius II shouldn't have taken up, literally, the sword." "Gregory XVI was wrong to oppose using gas to light Rome." This even applies to sainted popes: "Peter had it coming when Paul rebuked him to his face." "Celestine V was a holy but incompetent pope." And so on.

Such after-the-fact criticisms may be true and just or may be skewed and unfair. If the latter, you might be challenged to show proof of your characterization, but few will argue that you should not have said anything negative at all. Everyone agrees that a pope's coronation or installation doesn't change his human nature: he remains a sinner, even if we hope he always will act as a saint, and he certainly will not be omnicompetent, that being an attribute reserved to God alone. Any pope will have strengths and weaknesses, areas of deep understanding and areas of superficial understanding, attractive personal traits and unattractive personal traits. This is as true of live popes as of dead popes. Should there be no difference then in the ease with which a reigning pope may be criticized compared to a deceased pope, particularly one long deceased?

These are not easy considerations for conservatively-minded Catholics to deal with. Almost by instinct such folks are protective of the papacy. Those familiar with ecclesiastical history know—or at least they sense—that the Petrine office has been key in keeping the Church from going off the rails. "Confirm your brethren," Christ instructed Peter (Luke 22:32). The authority given to Peter, whose nickname means "Rock," is awe-full. It is Christ's own authority, given to Peter, as head of the apostles, in a way not given to the other apostles. Anyone who perceives this, as conservatively-minded Catholics do, will have an innate reluctance when it comes to voicing a complaint about any of Peter's successors, even those long-dead. Even the worst of them held an august office, and the best of them—many of the sainted popes but also many of those not yet sainted—demonstrated through their actions that the papacy was no mere human institution.

It is different with a non-Catholic. He will have no more hesitancy in criticizing a pope, living or dead, than he would have in criticizing a politician, living or dead. Why should he? Most of those who reject the authority of the papacy, whether they are Christians or not, think the institution really is little more than the product of centuries-long political machinations. Not a few Catholics think much the same, particularly those who style themselves progressive. (Some of their conservative counterparts would style them Modernists, harkening back to a term made famous by Pius X.) They see the papacy having, perhaps, a social or quasi-political utility, but they don't think of it as a locus of authority as such, the modern world for the most part not recognizing that authority any longer exists.

So, as I say, it commonly is not easy for conservatively-minded Catholics to criticize popes; it is something done more with reluctance than with alacrity. They see each pope not just as the Holy Father but as a father to them (analogously to seeing the Virgin Mary as a mother to them). A normal person hesitates before criticizing his father, particularly in public.

* * *

This book is subtitled "Why and How Conservative Catholics Squabble about Pope Francis." Let me explain what the subtitle hopes to convey.

"Why and How." Anyone who criticizes a reigning pope has a reason for making the criticism. It may be a good reason or a poor reason, a reasonable reason or an unreasonable reason. There may be one reason, or there may be a multiplicity of reasons. No one gives criticism where he thinks only praise is due. He criticizes because he perceives faults, whether great or small, numerous or few.

He criticizes because he seeks change. He wants the pope to cease doing whatever it is that makes for the criticism. He wants him to start doing A and to stop doing B. He hopes that by making criticisms public the result might be, if not papal reform, at least a better understanding of the problem among the critic's readers.

That's the "Why." If that were as far as I wished to go in these pages, then all I would need to do is to quote the critics, but my interest lies in more than just their criticisms, some of which I may think cogent, others partly so, still others not cogent at all. I also am interested in the "How": how do disputants carry on their disputes? How do they frame arguments, assuming they make identifiable arguments and don't satisfy themselves with mere posturing? Such questions make this book, in part, an investigation of rhetoric.

That too is a word that needs definition. In everyday parlance *rhetoric* connotes contentless argumentation. It has a purely negative sense. Someone accused of using rhetoric is accused of using argumentative words unfairly or unjustly. He may be speaking grandiloquently, but in fact he's just mouthing off. Rhetoric is used for show, for effect, for virtue signaling, but that is its extent.

No, not really. The term has a better pedigree than that. Historically rhetoric has been understood to be the art of persuasive speech. A syllogism, standing on its own, may not be persuasive. It may be perfectly logical, irrefutable on its own terms, and yet it may move no one to change his mind or behavior. Rhetoric uses syllogisms and other suasions to bring about a change of heart and of mind. Like nearly anything else, it can be abused, and it has been from its abuse that we have the modern connotation of the word.

Even in Classical times there was high rhetoric and there was low rhetoric—the rhetoric of the Roman Senate and the rhetoric of the Roman street. They overlapped but were identifiably distinct. We once enjoyed fairly high rhetoric in America, most notably in our politics, but few today will have images of the Roman Senate brought to mind when they read of the goings on in the United States Senate.

In these pages I want to look at how certain people who talk about Pope Francis do their talking—or, more precisely, their writing, since it will be to the written word that I will refer.

So this book proposes to look at the "Why" and "How" of people who criticize and defend the pope—but which people? My focus is on "Conservative Catholics." Immediately there is a problem, since *conservative* is a term more appropriate to politics than to religion. Why have I used it in the subtitle? Because I could think of no other word that would let prospective readers understand immediately which Catholics I propose to look at. I considered using *orthodox*, but there are orthodox Catholics who would not be considered conservative, either in politics or in their general religious outlook. Some might call them "everyday Catholics" or "middle of the road Catholics" or "mainstream Catholics." They accept the teachings of the Church, so far as they understand them, and they oppose no moral teachings, however much they may fail to live up to some of them, but the issues brought up in these pages are foreign to them. They know this pope and his predecessors only vaguely, from headlines or television news snippets, but they probably know more about the British royal family than they do about recent heads of their own Church.

So, if *orthodox* would be too broad, what term would be better, as a net wide enough to include the spectrum of views found in what follows? As I said, I could come up with no signpost better than *conservative*, though the term carries political baggage. In the following pages I will try to use it sparingly.

Now to the verb, "Squabble." I think it may be a *mot juste*. For the most part the exchanges of views among the parties here don't rise to authentic antagonisms, but often enough they evince the pettiness or persnicketiness that *squabble* can imply, though squabbling goes beyond such terms. What makes squabbling simultaneously frustrating and attractive is that it's something that happens within families. There is disagreement, sometimes profound, but also (though not always) affection and regard. Nearly all families know this. So it is within the Church. People who are close to one another on the spectrum may be less gentlemanly when they argue than people who are far apart—then again, they may be more cautious, not wanting to offend near neighbors. We find both tendencies.

That much for the subtitle. I should add a few words about the main title, *The Francis Feud*. I hope it succeeds in suggesting disagreement among people who write or speak about the pope and not that the pope himself is engaged in a feud. To be sure, Pope Francis has made allusions to his critics, but for the most part we can say that the disputes are *about* him yet don't *involve* him. He has shown a singular capacity to plant seeds that others nurture into disputes. (That is one complaint about him: his imprecisions invite others to reach conflicting interpretations of papal statements.)

Most discussions about the pope, at least by those who broadly fall under the rubric "conservative Catholics," have taken place online, partly in articles and blog posts, largely in comments that are appended to articles and blog posts. Not only has there been something of the ephemeral about the discussion—at least the part that hasn't been found within books, several of which are mentioned in the following pages—but the various parts of the discussion are strewn all over the place. Someone coming to it fresh might have difficulty tracking down the main lines of argument and the most representative arguers. I don't claim to have done that, even to my own satisfaction. No doubt I have overlooked much, and I admittedly have omitted much that has come to my attention. There are too many players, just counting the ones I am most familiar with, to give each even a short mention.

It is not my purpose to construct either a rogues gallery or a walk of fame, partly because I am no disinterested observer. I quote others at length. I also quote myself at length. Not only have I been privy to discussions, but I have been part of many of them. In the following pages I wear two hats: observer and participant. I see no reason to affect an impartiality that I don't have. If there has been a squabble concerning Pope Francis, I have played a role, if only as a secondary squabbler.

Most of my working years have been spent as a Catholic apologist. No one who dislikes the give and take of arguing enters apologetics either as a vocation or an avocation. (No one who dislikes swinging a club or a racket devotes time to golf or tennis.) I am constitutionally unable to view arguments without a critical eye. Even when I sympathize with a conclusion, I may deplore the way it was reached. Bad arguing rankles.

More than once during my apologetics career I have been tempted to take aside a foe of the Catholic Church and say, "Here, let me show you how to do it. I can make a more convincing argument for your side than you can." In this book I sometimes take aside friends who, in my estimation, have gone too far or have not gone far enough. I hope my disagreements with them are not taken as indications of diminished regard but as acknowledgments of the importance of the topics.

# Chapter 1

# The Anonymous Complainant

I read *The Dictator Pope* two weeks after it was published. On December 19, 2017, I wrote this synopsis of it on my Facebook timeline. I titled it "Is Pope Francis a Kitty Cat or an Autocrat?"

> I just finished reading *The Dictator Pope*, published under the pen name "Marcantonio Colonna." (The real Marcantonio Colonna was an admiral at the Battle of Lepanto.) At the moment the book is ranked #2,265 among all books sold at Amazon's Kindle Store, and it's ranked #2 in three categories, including "Popes & the Vatican"—this at two weeks after publication. Whatever else one wishes to say about it, the book is selling well, particularly at such a high price ($9.50) for such a slim work (141 print pages equivalent). An Italian version came out two weeks earlier and, naturally enough, isn't selling nearly as well at Amazon's American website.

What can one say about *The Dictator Pope*? I start with the unfortunate title. It's unfortunate in that it's only a step away from mere name-calling, and it tends to make the prospective reader suspect that the author is a crank. He doesn't come across that way when you read the book, but I do think the title was a blunder.

Likewise with the illustrations that appear in the middle of the book. The first is a pair of head shots of Pope Francis. In one he is half smiling and has wide eyes. In the others he is straight-lipped and is looking out the corners of his eyes. The caption is "Which is the real Francis?" This is a juvenile tactic. There follow a dozen photos of "bad guys" (cardinals, bishops, and priests) and six photos of "good guys" (including Cardinals [Raymond] Burke, [Robert] Sarah, and [Gerhard] Müller). The captions for the "bad guys" are tendentious. It would have been better to leave out the captions entirely—or, better yet, to leave out the photos entirely.

Others who have reviewed the book have noted that, while most of the author's assertions are sufficiently grounded, some are not, and a few seem fanciful. The author is described at Amazon as "a graduate of Oxford University [who] has extensive experience of historical and other research," but the book is chiefly a gathering of stories and comments that already appeared elsewhere. There isn't anything to suggest that the author actually is a historian or that he has done original research.

The chief service done by the book is to put in one place reminders of things the pope has said and done not just while pope but earlier, while in Argentina. Some of the claims of the book are not well sourced. That said, there is sufficient information here to conclude that Pope Francis is a kind of pope the Church has not seen in several centuries: an ecclesiastical politician with a Tammany Hall flavor. The author says, "Some of the modern popes have been great men, other have been adequate; for centuries there has been none who was, as one must say brutally of Francis, so plainly beneath his office." That's a harsh judgment, but it's not an unfair judgment, given what the author collects in these pages.

There seems to be considerable buyer's remorse among cardinals who were in the 2013 conclave. Most thought they were electing a reformist pope, but little has been reformed. The author's gripes are not so much about what Pope Francis believes or the positions he seems to be promoting—the book isn't titled *The Heretic Pope*—but about his machinations, his heavy-handedness, his making end runs around long-established procedures, his surrounding himself with yes-men (some of them simply incompetent), his persistent scolding and the consequent loss of morale that has induced in Vatican personnel both clerical and lay.

There isn't much in the book that I hadn't seen elsewhere, though I hadn't seen the claim that at the conclave Cardinal Bergoglio received 95 votes (out of about 120 total). It's hard to tell what that means. It takes two-thirds (about 80 votes) to elect a man pope. When a cardinal shows momentum through several ballots, often it's been the case that the conclavists realize what the result is likely to be and so most of them jump on the bandwagon in order to approximate unanimity.

We don't know how the voting went in 2013, but if the Argentine cardinal received progressively 40, then 50, then 60 votes, with runners-up indicating that they'd like to bow out, then I could imagine that, at the end, another 35 added their (reluctant) votes to wrap things up. Or maybe the number 95 indicates how many cardinal electors really were happy to vote for the Argentine. If they haven't become disillusioned—the author thinks that many of them have—then, when the papal throne again is vacant, it's possible that a Francis Redux might be elected. Or the disillusionment might be so great that the electors will look for someone not associated with this pope's administration. Who knows?

I think *The Dictator Pope* would have been a better book if the author had had a good editor. It's not so much that he needed someone to fix up his writing. He's a pretty good writer. But he needed someone to tell him that this, that, and the other thing either were not sufficiently proved or were phrased too frenetically. He also needed someone to insist that he get behind the secondary sources that he too much relies on. Weaknesses such as these make the book less influential or useful than it might have been.

One last point. I think Marcantonio Colonna should have used his real name. Apparently the Vatican is trying to determine his identity, and, in a written interview, Colonna said that he expects to be outed eventually and that the process likely will bring the book even more attention. That may be so, but I think that's too calculating by half. He should have just used his real name.

I don't know who he is. He might be someone of stature, or he might be a nobody who feared that by using his real name the book would be ignored as being from, well, a nobody. I'd be surprised if he doesn't turn out to be the latter. However that may be, and however inadequate *The Dictator Pope* is at several levels, it's good that it's been published—not so much for what it is in itself but because it may induce better scholars, writers, and commentators to do work in the same field.

So that was my Facebook post. As I said, at that time I wasn't aware of the true identity of Marcantonio Colonna. Later the author was revealed to be Henry Sire, who also is published as H. J. A. Sire. I didn't recall his name, but when I looked him up I realized I had on my shelves two other books of his, both as yet unread by me. One is a biography of Fr. Martin D'Arcy. I bought it because D'Arcy was a friend of one of my favorite writers, Msgr. Ronald Knox. The other book is *Phoenix from the Ashes: The Making, Unmaking, and Restoration of Catholic Tradition.* It is described at Amazon as "a comprehensive look at the state of the Catholic Church since the Second Vatican Council," and the promotional blurbs on the back cover make it clear that it is written from a Traditionalist perspective.

Is Sire "someone of stature" or, as I speculated, "a nobody who feared that by using his real name the book would be ignored as being from, well, a nobody"? I think it would be fair to say that he is neither: he is neither well known in Catholic circles (even if known to a fair number of Traditionalists) nor is he a nobody. His new publisher says Sire was born in Barcelona, attended Stonyhurst (a Jesuit school) and Oxford, where he obtained a degree in history. Two years ago his official history of the Knights of Malta was published: *The Knights of Malta: A Modern Resurrection.* It was an update of a book he wrote in 1996 and seems to have been his last substantial engagement with the Knights, for, when his authorship of *The Dictator Pope* was made public, the Knights asked him to resign from the organization, which he did.

\* \* \*

Others took note of *The Dictator Pope* around the same time I did.

Writing at the Catholic World Report website, Phil Lawler, author of *Lost Shepherd*—another book critical of Pope Francis—said of Colonna's book, "[W]hen the book told stories that were new to me, I found the evidence thin. Too often the author relies on hearsay evidence, and when he cites other reporters, too often their work is based on hearsay as well. Worse, when he makes his most startling claims, Colonna offers no evidence at all. He makes the improbable claim, for example, that then-Cardinal Bergoglio had advance notice about the impending resignation of Pope Benedict XVI, when many of the former Pontiff's closest advisers were taken by surprise. Later he makes the even more outlandish charge that Pope Francis used the proceeds of the Peter's Pence collection to subsidize the presidential campaign of Hillary Clinton. Very few readers will be ready to accept these claims without some persuasive evidence. By putting them forward as facts, without supporting them, the author encourages readers to wonder about the book's other claims."[4]

Commenting on Lawler's piece online, R. J. Stove, an Australian who has written biographies of Palestrina and

César Franck, opined that Colonna "has destroyed his own credibility" by using a pseudonym. Carl E. Olson, editor of Catholic World Report, demurred, saying, "'Destroyed' is a pretty strong word in this context. Having read the book, I'd say that it, especially as a record of this pontificate's many problems, stands on its own strengths and weaknesses. In a way, actually, using a pseudonym might end up being a smart strategy, as there are credible reports that Francis's allies are seeking to 'out' the author. That, I think, will bring much more attention to both the book and to the tactics employed by Francis and Co."[5] Olson may be right about that: the search for Colonna might have given his book more publicity than it otherwise would have received.

Writing as one contributor among 45 in a *Catholic World Report* round-up titled "The Best Books I Read in 2017," James Kalb said, "Apart from the Bible and saints' lives, most of the Catholic books I read this year had to do with contentious issues. The most contentious was *The Dictator Pope*, by the pseudonymous Marcantonio Colonna. I read it shortly after reading several very positive books about Francis and his pontificate and was ready for something that would round out the favorable interpretations with a compilation of information—mostly publicly available, but some apparently from the author's contacts in the Vatican—that supports more troubling interpretations that can't be shrugged off. As far as I could tell, the book performed its task competently."[6]

\* \* \*

Robert Royal had published a review of *The Dictator Pope* at The Catholic Thing on December 6, 2017.[7] He is the editor in chief of the website, which began in 2008 and is described as "a forum for intelligent Catholic commentary." When the website launched, Royal wrote, "Our mission is to bring the best Catholic thought and action into the public square."[8] This was to be done by gathering bespoke writings from prominent (and not so prominent) Catholics whose material otherwise would not appear in one venue.

> All of our columnists write frequently in other places, but there is no one place where you will find them all together offering material unavailable elsewhere. Wide-ranging and solid Catholic commentary on events is necessary, not only to keep us from being overwhelmed by the tsunami of information now coming at us all from many sources, but to cast a steady and invigorating Catholic light on what is otherwise a superficial and dull world.

Royal holds a Ph.D. in comparative literature from Catholic University of America. In the 1980s and 1990s he served as vice president of George Weigel's Washington-based Ethics and Public Policy Center, and he now serves as president of the Faith & Reason Institute, which he founded. He has written numerous books. The biographical entry[9] on him at Wikipedia says he "is generally conservative and a critic of secularism." Given Royal's earlier associations, it might be accurate to say that he was, and perhaps still may be, a neo-conservative in politics. At any rate, he universally is considered orthodox in his Catholicism and has not had the reputation of being a firebrand. With Raymond Arroyo and Fr. Gerald Murray, Royal appears on EWTN in its "Papal Posse" commentary segment.

For now, let's have Royal speak for himself, as he takes his first public notice of *The Dictator Pope*.

> The title above is the name of a book that appeared Monday in English (after earlier publication in Italian) by a writer who has assumed a grand Renaissance pseudonym: Marcantonio Colonna (an admiral at Lepanto). He evidently could not publish under his real name, for fear of reprisals. But the case he lays out is largely convincing: that Pope Francis has carefully cultivated an image in public as the apostle of mercy, kindness, and openness; in private, he's authoritarian, given to profanity-laced outbursts of anger, and manipulative in pursuing his agenda.

The last part of the last sentence reflects the views of both the author of *The Dictator Pope* and Robert Royal, but the three claims have not been equally demonstrated. The first—that Francis is authoritarian—needs to be established on the basis of an overarching view of how he operates. The term *authoritarian* is a loaded one. It has a proper use in political science, psychology, and elsewhere, but it ought to be applied only when an authoritarian tendency is not just spotted but is pronounced and repetitive.

I suppose at some point Mother Teresa, when dealing with one of her sisters, may have lost her patience, thus permitting a witness to conclude that, in that one instance, Mother Teresa acted in an authoritarian manner, but an isolated slip (the kind of thing we all are prone to) is insufficient to characterize a character, just as the fact (if it was a fact) that Stalin was kind to his chauffeur doesn't negate the fact (which certainly was a fact) that he was an authoritarian.

So, for the time being, let's set aside the label of "authoritarian" for Francis. What about "manipulative"? This will be a label easier to apply, I think, as we work through the views and discussions that appear in the following pages. And what about the third description, that Francis is "given to profanity-laced outbursts of anger"? I don't know whether Royal has independent evidence of this, but Colonna failed to substantiate his charge. It would be nice to think that no pope, whether this one or any other, ever uses profane language, and I work on the presumption that perhaps none of the popes of my lifetime ever have done so, even before stepping into Peter's shoes. But we do know, in times long past, that there were popes whose failings in office were more serious than merely a profane tongue. So, it's possible that Colonna is correct in his charge, but, absent substantiation, who can say? (It is not enough to say, "Where there's smoke, there's fire," to assert that if charges of the pope's profanity are widespread—for the sake of this argument, let's assume they are—then there must be some truth, some occurrences, behind them. Not necessarily. Sometimes, where there's smoke, there's only smoke.)

> This is hardly news, least of all in Rome. This volume, however, is far more probing and detailed than anything that has previously appeared. It sometimes stretches evidence, but the sheer amount of evidence it provides is stunning. About 90 percent of it is simply incontrovertible and cannot help but clarify who Francis is and what he's about.

Here Royal gives Colonna some leash. Many critics of *The Dictator Pope* don't. It is easy enough to find poorly substantiated claims in the book—the pope's alleged profanity is but one example—and some defenders of Francis hardly look beyond the book's weaknesses when writing their reviews. They make little attempt to discuss whether "90 percent of it is simply incontrovertible." They don't ask themselves whether Colonna, who gets some things wrong or who fails to prove some things, might not have highlighted true shortcomings of this papacy. They focus on the writer's weak points and sidestep his strong points—easy to do when a book has a few glaring weaknesses.

The parts of this story I know best—the synods on the family that I reported on daily from Rome for TCT [The Catholic Thing]—are absolutely reliable. We know, for example, that Pope Francis was quite willing to openly manipulate the synods by personally appointing supporters of the Kasper Proposal and that he even intervened personally at key points, changing procedures and instructing the bishops about where their deliberations should start—and end.

When Francis cares about something—as Colonna shows—he makes it happen, whatever the opposition (at the synods, it was considerable). There's a clear pattern of behavior, whatever uncertainties remain. On the divorced and remarried, the environment, immigrants, "Islamophobia," the poor, the pope is relentless. But he was not elected to revolutionize marital doctrine or "discipline." Nor was he chosen to be a player in international politics. He was elected to be a "reformer" who would mainly clean up Vatican finances and deal with the gay lobby, two things that played a role in Benedict's resignation.

On the financial front, there was a strong start: the council of cardinals, Cardinal [George] Pell's effort to inject Anglo-Saxon transparency, a new special secretariat on the economy, hiring PriceWaterhouseCoopers to do an external audit. The momentum stalled as the old guard slowly regained control over Vatican finances—and oversight. A series of Vatican Bank presidents, officials, accountants, etc.—probably getting too close to the truth—have been fired without good explanations. (Something similar played out in the Knights of Malta controversy.) Pell had to return to Australia to deal with sexual abuse charges from forty years ago that, suspiciously, resurfaced after being earlier examined and dismissed.

And where was the pope during all of this? He didn't seem very interested. If he had been, he'd be at least as dogged in dealing with financial reform as he is, say, about global warming. Austen Ivereigh, a British writer and papal fan, entitled his biography *The Great Reformer*, in part because of Jorge Bergoglio's alleged role in curbing abuses in Buenos Aires. Colonna doubts the truth of that account, and not only because of Francis's lack of action in Rome. He thinks the Argentinian stories should be re-examined.

Then there's the gay mafia. People forget that the occasion for Francis's famous remark "Who am I to judge?" was not a general comment about homosexuality. It was in response to a question about Msgr. Battista Ricca, who was involved in several notorious homosexual scandals, some right across the river from Buenos Aires in Uruguay. Nonetheless, right after the 2013 papal election, he became the pope's "eyes and ears" at the Vatican Bank and director of the Casa Santa Marta, where Francis resides.

And then there's the troubling, casual resurrection of figures like Cardinal Gottfried Daneels, once thoroughly discredited for his support for contraception, divorce, gay marriage, even euthanasia and abortion—and outrageous mishandling of priestly abuse. But he stood with Francis on the balcony of St. Peter's right after the conclave and read the prayer for the new pope at his inauguration. He was also one of the ringers Francis personally invited to bolster his case at the synods.

Then there's the appointment of another radical, Archbishop [Vincenzo] Paglia, to head the "reformed" John Paul II Institute on Marriage and the Family. In a remarkably naked authoritarian move, the pope substituted himself for Cardinal [Robert] Sarah for the Institute's opening academic address in 2016 and spoke of "a far too abstract and almost artificial theological ideal of marriage." You have to believe that Cardinal [Reinhard] Marx was expressing the truth when he said, at the end of the synods, that it was just the beginning.

The least satisfactory part of this book for me is the account of how the "St. Gallen Group"—one of its own members called it a "mafia"—which met to plan opposition to St. JPII [John Paul II] and Joseph Ratzinger, identified Jorge Bergoglio as a future papal candidate. He had no global visibility until he gave the concluding address at the 2001 synod on the role of bishops. NYC's Cardinal Edward Egan was supposed to do that but stayed home because 9/11 had just happened. The address impressed the synod fathers for its fairness to both sides. Colonna reveals, however, that it was entirely the work of a synod secretary/speechwriter, Msgr. Daniel Emilio Estivill. We need to know more about how things went, from then to now.

Colonna also weakens his credibility somewhat by repeating rumors that Vatican Secretary of State Cardinal [Pietro] Parolin convinced Francis to use money from Peter's Pence to support Hillary Clinton's presidential campaign. No footnotes appear to support this claim, nor does Colonna offer a plausible account of how and why Rome would think Mrs. Clinton—Hillary Clinton?—worth such a risky bet and potential scandal.

This undoubtedly is the weakest claim in *The Dictator Pope*, that Francis's Vatican would intervene financially in a foreign election. Colonna offers no substantiation. Had this and a few other poorly-established claims been dropped from the book, and had its title been different, it's likely that the book would have had a better reception and a wider readership.

Despite a few lapses, the most disturbing element remains: the abundant evidence—confirmed by many particular instances now over years of this papacy—that the pope has little use for established procedures, precedents, even legal structures within the Church. These are not mere trivial rules, Pharisaic legalism, resistance to the Holy Spirit, etc. They are the means by which the Church seeks to be clear, fair, and orderly—and to address unjust actions or abuses by those in power.

When the head of the Church himself does not much feel bound by the tradition or impartial laws he has inherited, what then? That the question even has to be asked is disturbing. Any answer will have to reckon with the eye-opening material in this compelling book.

One thing to notice about Royal's review of *The Dictator Pope* is that it says almost nothing about doctrine. Royal doesn't allege that Pope Francis is attempting to alter Church teaching. (Henry Sire, the real name behind "Marcantonio Colonna," does think that of Francis.) Royal is concerned not so much about what Francis teaches but about how he governs. As we will see, the case for Francis supposedly wanting to change doctrine is not particularly strong, and it hardly extends beyond the issue of Communion for the divorced and remarried.

\* \* \*

Steve Skojec runs the website OnePeterFive. The title refers to 1 Peter 5, the eighth and ninth verses of which read: "Be sober, be watchful. Your adversary the devil prowls around like a roaring lion, seeking someone to devour. Resist him, firm in your faith, knowing that the same experience of suffering is required of your brotherhood throughout the world." This sense of resistance seems to be the defining note of the website, which Skojec describes this way:

> OnePeterFive exists as a place to begin rebuilding the Catholic ethos. We're not just here to zero in on the problems, but to offer concrete solutions. We want to restore Catholic culture, rebuild the Church as a patron of the arts, reinvigorate the family and the traditions that keep it strong, reform the liturgy, support vocations, dust off the old devotions and make them relevant again.[10]

The website lists about two dozen "featured contributors," but Skojec writes about half of the articles. He has a bachelor's degree in communications and theology from Franciscan University of Steubenville. He and most of his contributors rightly could be labeled Traditionalist Catholics, though some contributors more properly should be labeled as conservative or traditional, but not Traditionalist, Catholics.

On November 30, 2017, Skojec uploaded what may

have been the earliest public notice of the English version of *The Dictator Pope*.[11]

> OnePeterFive has obtained an advance copy of the English text, and I am still working my way through it. Although most of its contents will be at least cursorily familiar to those who have followed this unusual pontificate, it treats in detail many of the most important topics we have covered in these pages, providing the additional benefit of collecting them all in one place. . . .
>
> The level of potential controversy associated with the book has seemingly led some journalists in Rome to be wary of broaching the book's existence publicly (though it is said to be very much a topic of private conversation), whether for fear of retribution—the Vatican has recently been known to exclude or mistreat journalists it suspects of hostility—or for some other reason, remains unclear.
>
> Notable exceptions to this conspicuous silence include the stalwart Marco Tosatti—who has already begun unpacking the text at his website, Stilum Curae—and Professor Roberto de Mattei, who writes that the book confirms Cardinal Müller's recent remarks that there is a "magic circle" around the pope which "prevents an open and balanced debate on the doctrinal problems raised" by objections like the *dubia* and Filial

Correction, and that there is also "a climate of espionage and delusion" in Francis's Vatican.

Some sources have even told me that the Vatican, incensed by the book's claims, is so ardently pursuing information about the author's true identity that they've been seeking out and badgering anyone they think might have knowledge of the matter. The Italian version of the book's website has already gone down since its launch. The reason, as one particularly credible rumor has it, is that its disappearance was a result of the harassment of its designer, even though that person had nothing to do with the book other than having been hired to put it online.

If these sound like thuggish tactics, the book wastes no time in confirming that this pope—and those who support him—are not at all above such things. Colonna introduces his text by way of an ominous portrait of Francis himself, describing a "miraculous change that has taken over" Bergoglio since his election—a change that Catholics of his native Buenos Aires noticed immediately: "Their dour, unsmiling archbishop was turned overnight into the smiling, jolly Pope Francis, the idol of the people with whom he so fully identifies. If you speak to anyone working in the Vatican, they will tell you about the miracle in reverse. When the publicity cameras are off him, Pope Francis turns into a different figure: arrogant, dismissive of people, prodigal of bad language and notorious for furious outbursts of temper which are known to everyone from the cardinals to the chauffeurs."

As mentioned when looking at Robert Royal's review of *The Dictator Pope*, here we have another example of the author's wide claims and thin substantiation. He says that Francis is "prodigal of bad language and notorious for furious outbursts of temper." Maybe he is, but an *ipse dixit* proves nothing, and this is the kind of claim that ought not to be made unless some sort of corroboration can be given. Granted, if low-level members of the papal household are sworn at by the pope, they hardly are likely to speak on the record about it. A laid-off papal chauffeur may not be able to find as lucrative a chauffeuring job elsewhere—or any at all. A man with a family to support may have to hunker down and continue in unhappy employment, knowing perhaps that the average papal reign has been seven years and that he might find his next boss to be more congenial.

All that acknowledged, the airiness of some of Colonna's claims is disconcerting. There may be times when you might have a moral certainty that something is so but you have no way to prove it to the public, so all you can do is wait, keeping what you know in reserve. If you broadcast what you can't prove, you might do little more than undercut those claims you can prove. I suspect that may have happened with *The Dictator Pope*. Had the half-a-dozen least substantiated claims been omitted, the book might have lost none of its force.

Colonna writes, too, of the "buyer's remorse" that some of the cardinals who elected Bergoglio are experiencing as his pontificate approaches its fifth anniversary: "Francis is showing," writes Colonna, "that he is not the democratic, liberal ruler that the cardinals thought they were electing in 2013 but a papal tyrant the like of whom has not been seen for many centuries."

Colonna then transitions to an opening chapter exposing the work of the so-called St. Gallen "Mafia"—the group of cardinals who had been conspiring for decades to see to it that a pope of their liking—a pope like Cardinal Jorge Mario Bergoglio was capable of becoming—would be elected. Formed in 1996 (with precursor meetings between progressive European prelates giving initial shape to the group as early as the 1980s) in St. Gallen, Switzerland, the St. Gallen Mafia was originally headed up by the infamous late archbishop of Milan, Cardinal Carlo Maria Martini.

The group roster was a rogue's gallery of heterodox prelates with a list of ecclesiastical accomplishments that reads more like a rap sheet than a curriculum vitae. (In the case of Godfried Daneels, implicated in some way in about 50 of 475 dossiers on clerical sexual abuse allegations that mysteriously disappeared after evidence seized by Belgian police was inexplicably declared inadmissible in court, this comparison transcends analogy.)

Here Skojec uses language that not a few Traditionalists fall into repeatedly. Carlo Maria Martini wasn't just the late archbishop of Milan: he was "the infamous late archbishop." Members of the St. Gallen Mafia weren't just liberal prelates. They were "heterodox prelates" who formed not just a group but "a rogue's gallery." Their deeds read like "a rap sheet." It is this kind of language that makes non-Traditionalist eyes roll. None of these terms adds substance or confidence to Skojec's characterizations. What is accomplished by terming Martini "infamous"? Less than Skojec imagines. The label doesn't establish Martini's infamy, but it does tell the reader that Skojec doesn't like him. It also tells the reader that Skojec may be incapable of looking at his opponents with anything but biased spectacles.

> The names of some of the most prominent members of the group—many of which would have been unknown to even relatively well-informed Catholics just a decade ago—have become uncomfortably familiar in recent years: Cardinals Martini, Daneels, Kasper, [Karl] Lehmann, and [Jerome] Murphy-O'Connor have all risen in profile considerably since their protege was elevated to the Petrine throne.

After a controversial career, Walter Kasper had already begun fading into obscurity before he was unexpectedly praised in the new pope's first Angelus address on March 17, 2013. Francis spoke admiringly of Kasper's book on the topic of mercy—a theme that would become a defining touchstone of his pontificate. When Kasper was subsequently tapped to present the keynote at the February 14, 2014, consistory of cardinals, the advancement of his proposal to create a path for Communion for the divorced and remarried thrust him further into the spotlight.

The so-called "Kasper Proposal" launched expectations for the two synods that would follow on marriage and the family and provided the substrate for the post-synodal apostolic exhortation, *Amoris Laetitia*, around which there has been a theological and philosophical debate the likes of which has not seen in the living memory of the Church. For his part, Daneels, who retired from his position as archbishop of Brussels under "a cloud of scandal" in 2010, even went so far as to declare that the 2013 conclave result represented for him "a personal resurrection experience."

And what was the goal of the St. Gallen group? Originally, their agenda was to bring about a "much more modern" Church. That goal finally crystallized around opposition to the anticipated election of Cardinal Joseph Ratzinger to the papacy—a battle in which they were narrowly defeated during the 2005 conclave, when, according to an undisclosed source within the curia, the penultimate ballot showed a count of 40 votes for Bergoglio and 72 for Ratzinger. Colonna cites German Catholic journalist Paul Badde in saying that it was the late Cardinal Joachim Meisner—later one of the four *dubia* cardinals—who "passionately fought" the St. Gallen Mafia in favor of the election of Ratzinger. After this loss, the St. Gallen Mafia officially disbanded.

But although Cardinal Martini died in 2012, they staged a comeback—and eventually won the day—on Wednesday, March 13, 2013. For it was on that day that Jorge Mario Bergoglio stepped out onto the loggia of St. Peter's Basilica, victorious, as Pope Francis the First. Those paying attention would take note that one Cardinal Gottfried Daneels of Belgium stood triumphantly by his side. . . .

From this analysis of Francis' inauspicious beginnings as the handpicked pope of the most progressive forces in the Church, Colonna takes us on a brief but informative tour of his life and background. He mentions Bergoglio's strained relationship with his parents—his father a "struggling accountant" and mother a temporary invalid—noting that he rarely speaks of them. He examines Bergoglio's precipitous rise through the

Jesuits in Argentina, despite opposition from his superiors at certain critical points along the way.

Highlighted too, was the assessment of the unusually young provincial by the Jesuit Superior General—offered when Bergoglio applied for a dispensation from the Jesuit rule forbidding him from becoming a bishop—allegedly describing him in no uncertain terms as unsuitable for the role. I say allegedly, because the text of the evaluation has never been made public.

Writes Colonna: "Father [Peter Hans] Kolvenbach accused Bergoglio of a series of defects, ranging from habitual use of vulgar language to deviousness, disobedience concealed under a mask of humility, and lack of psychological balance; with a view to his suitability as a future bishop, the report pointed out that he had been a divisive figure as provincial of his own order. It is not surprising that, on being elected pope, Francis made efforts to get his hands on the existing copies of the document, and the original filed in the official Jesuit archives in Rome has disappeared."

This claim about the Kolvenbach report may be true—or not. If true, it seems to be an authentic discovery by Colonna. But, again, where is the substantiation? Kolvenbach died in 2016. Who might be able to verify

Colonna's representation? It's hard to say, since Colonna makes no attempt to prove what he says here.

> Despite these setbacks, Bergoglio was seen, at the time, as a champion of Catholic conservatism in the mode of John Paul II by Cardinal [Antonio] Quarracino, his predecessor in the archbishopric of Buenos Aires and the man who ultimately ignored the warnings and raised him to the episcopacy. The perception of Bergoglio's conservatism appears to have stemmed largely from his opposition to the Marxist liberation theology that had become so prevalent in the region. . . .

His Perónism helps to make clear, in another illuminating moment, Francis's infuriating habit of saying diametrically opposing things from one day to the next:

"The story is told that Perón, in his days of glory, once proposed to induct a nephew in the mysteries of politics. He first brought the young man with him when he received a deputation of communists; after hearing their views, he told them, 'You're quite right.' The next day he received a deputation of fascists and replied again to their arguments, 'You're quite right.' Then he asked his nephew what he thought and the young man said, 'You've spoken with two groups with diametrically opposite opinions and you told them both that you agreed with them. This is completely unacceptable.' Perón replied, 'You're quite right too.'

"An anecdote like this is an illustration of why no one can be expected to assess Pope Francis unless he understands the tradition of Argentinian politics, a phenomenon outside the rest of the world's experience; the Church has been taken by surprise by Francis because it has not had the key to him: he is Juan Perón in ecclesiastical translation. Those who seek to interpret him otherwise are missing the only relevant criterion."

The book is packed with such fascinating insights into the phenomena of the Francis papacy, in part by viewing the present through the lens of his past. From indications that his notorious simplicity was simply a means of shedding any "ballast" that might impede his pursuit of power to his ostentatious humility (often with cameras conveniently waiting to capture the moment) to his masterful manipulation of an over-eager media into displaying the image he wishes to portray, the layers of the Argentinian pope are peeled back and examined, offering a deeper understanding of the man himself.

Colonna does not spend much time on the question of the validity of Francis' papal election, but he does raise questions about the convenient (for the St. Gallen group) timing of Benedict's abdication and considerations made both by papal biographer Austen Ivereigh and Vatican journalist Antonio Socci on the politicking and the questionable canonical validity, respectively, in the 2013 conclave. "Whether one chooses to uphold Socci's view or not," Colonna writes, "there is something rather appropriate in the fact that the political heir of Juan Perón should have been raised to the head of the Catholic Church by what was arguably an invalid vote."

Here is another unpursued weakness in Colonna's book—and in Skojec's review of it. Both men seem open to the possibility that the 2013 conclave failed to effect a valid election. Not a single cardinal who was present, not even any of those who have been demoted or shunted aside by Francis, has suggested that the election was invalid. This notion seems to be raised only because Benedict XVI is still around. If, for sake of argument, the election of Francis failed (meaning he would be an anti-pope: apparently a pope but not really a pope), then either the papacy is vacant or Benedict still is pope.

The latter would be a possibility, opine such people, if there was a failure on Benedict's part too: if he failed to effect a resignation. Just as it is possible for a baptism to be invalid if the Trinitarian formula is not used contemporaneously with the application of water, so it would be possible for Benedict—this is the theory—to think he was resigning while failing to accomplish a resignation because of the use of inadequate or too-vague wording. And if all that had occurred—if Benedict's resignation didn't "take"—then he still would be pope and the conclave election would be void, even if all the electors thought it was valid.

Or, if Benedict's resignation did "take," the election might have been ineffectual for reasons that have not been made public. But if there were such reasons, why wouldn't a few electors—at least those later on the outs with Francis—have said something?

The book does not merely content itself with the pre-pontificate history of Bergoglio. Under the microscope, too, are the critical agenda items of the ongoing papacy, foremost among them those promises which have never materialized. From reform of the curia to a supposed "zero tolerance" policy on clerical sexual abusers to Vatican bank and financial reform, some of the major initiatives of the Francis papacy have failed to reach fruition, been abandoned, or have received only lip service.

Later chapters deal, among other important topics, with the heavily-manipulated synods on the family, the Vatican response to orthodox resistance, the saga surrounding the *dubia*, the gutting and reinvention of the Pontifical Academy for Life, the destruction of the Franciscan Friars of the Immaculate, the Vaticansupported coup within the Knights of Malta, and the persecution of those ecclesiastics who fail to toe the line for the papal agenda—along with an examination of the KGB-style tactics deployed by "Kremlin Santa Marta."

(On a personal note [writes Skojec], I was both pleased and honored to discover a chapter subheading entitled "The Dictatorship of Mercy," with a direct reference to the article in which I coined the term.)

There is a great deal of material in this book for all Catholics, but it will be of particular interest to readers of this website, who have watched many of these developments unfold in real time. There are also new things to learn from the text, particularly in its examination of the pope's Argentinian history. If you or someone you know is interested in getting up to speed quickly on where things are with this papacy—and why it is so singularly controversial—this book appears to be an excellent starting point to cover much of the necessary ground. At 141 pages, it provides a sufficient amount of depth without overwhelming the reader with too much information, and the language and presentation make it an easy, fascinating read.

\* \* \*

Two weeks after OnePeterFive first mentioned *The Dictator Pope*, LifeSite News published an interview with Marcantonio Colonna.[12] The interview was conducted by Diane Montagna, a regular contributor to the website.

Asked why he wrote *The Dictator Pope*, Colonna—later revealed to be Henry Sire, but I will use the pseudonym here—answered, "The popular image of Pope Francis is one of the most extraordinary deceptions of the present time and contrasts totally with the reality of Bergoglio's character as it was known in Argentina before his election and is known in the Vatican today. My aim was to let the cat out of the bag and to set out, in a series of studies of policies followed over the past five years, the true nature of Francis's pontificate. . . . [W]hat I principally had in mind was trying to avoid a similar mistake being made again in the next conclave. My aim was to expose the myth of the supposedly liberal pope who was elected in 2013 and to urge the cardinals at the next conclave to avoid electing an unknown figure who turns out to be quite different from what he had been thought."

Montagna asked Colonna why he didn't work out of the public eye, sending his long report (the book runs to 60,000 words) privately to the cardinals, the future papal electors. In this her question anticipated comments by defenders of the pope who wrote in the following weeks, arguing that it is not necessary for any Catholic to complain about or reprimand a pope in public and that all such actions should be undertaken in private, if at all. Colonna said he went public because he could not reasonably expect most cardinals to read such a long book without external promptings and because "the book needs to have the credibility that comes from having been made public and recognized as true by those who know the Vatican."

Asked his overall view of the pope, Colonna said, "My view of Pope Francis is mainly formed from researching his Argentinian background. He emerges as a flawed character who is capable of impressing people profoundly and forming warm friendships but who, as one of his priest friends remarked, 'manipulates people through the affections.' This characteristic has enabled him to establish a skillful ascendancy over his subordinates in Rome, as he had done previously in Buenos Aires. Bergoglio is also very much the product of the peculiar political culture of Argentina, formed by the populist dictator Juan Perón, of whom Bergoglio was a follower from his early years and whom he very much resembles in his style of government."

Montagna noted that most of Colonna's claims are footnoted, but a prominent exception stands out: the charge that under Francis the Vatican attempted to help Hillary Clinton's presidential campaign by transferring money to it. Asked why he included this item, Colonna said, "This accusation was made to me unambiguously by a contact in the Vatican, whose identity I have to protect. However, the allegation is quite well known to journalists. With this and other scandals I mention, my desire was to encourage further investigation by researchers who are better qualified than I am to delve into financial matters."

This strikes me as a journalistic blunder. Accusations ought not to be thrown out merely in hopes that someone will take the lead and conduct necessary research. That someone made the accusation "unambiguously" tells us nothing more than that the person was convinced of the truth of what he was saying; it doesn't mean that what he thought was true really was. By printing such a claim—without source, citation, or proof—Colonna undercut trust in the rest of his narrative, most of which is little more than a compilation of stories published scattershot over the first five years of Francis's reign.

Colonna's other chief blunder was his choice of title. The word "dictator" is incendiary rather than explanatory, and the evidence Colonna serves up, even if it all proves accurate, hardly amounts to Francis being a dictator in the normal connotation of the term. Given the twentieth century's political history, which has spilled over into the twenty-first century, "dictator" conjures up certain images that are inapplicable to the case at hand. Colonna could have used a lesser term of disapproval, such as "autocrat," which doesn't carry so much baggage, or he could have used a still more anodyne—and, more importantly, more accurate—term.

As an author, I understand the allure of using a title that will grab prospective buyers' attention, but—and this is particularly true with non-fiction—the title ought to be accurate and not misleading. Hyperbole is not an author's friend, at least not in titling. In traditional publishing, the choice of title often is out of the author's hands. The book contract leaves that decision to the publisher and its marketing department. Not infrequently this results in a disconnect between the cover and the contents. But Colonna's book was not published traditionally. It was self-published through Amazon's Kindle Direct Publishing. He wrote the text, he edited the text, he laid out the text, and he designed the cover. (The cover clearly is the work of an amateur.) He had no check on his titling impulses, which is too bad. The same could be said regarding the words behind the cover: they could have used other pairs of eyes, to catch the hyperboles and infelicities.

Despite missteps such as these—and, perhaps because of them, at least in the choice of the title—*The Dictator Pope* held high rankings at Amazon, where it was available as an ebook. As late as seven weeks after publication of the English version, the book held the number-one spot in the category of "Popes & the Vatican," ahead of two books on John Paul II by Paul Kengor and George Weigel, and the number-two spot in two other categories. It was among the 9,000 top-selling ebooks at Amazon, out of several million.

Better comparisons would be to two other books that appeared in 2017 and were critical of the pope. *The Political Pope*, by George Neumayr, at this writing ranks 66 in the category of "Popes & the Vatican," and *Pope Francis in Context*, by E. Michael Jones, ranks 459 in the same category. Neumayr's book appeared in May, and Jones's book appeared in June. No doubt they had higher rankings six weeks after their debuts, but neither achieved the long-lasting top-of-the-heap ranking that *The Dictator Pope* has received.

Jones self-publishes his books, which are edited atrociously (lots of typographical and formatting errors) and feature covers that lack all artistic skill. It may be no wonder, then, that his book on Pope Francis languishes, but so does Neumayr's.

Colonna's book has a cover that isn't much better than the one on Jones's book, yet his book flourishes, at least for the time being, even though Colonna is (purposefully) an unknown, while Jones has a highly loyal if small following—he publishes *Culture Wars* magazine—and Neumayr has name recognition in several areas, both political and religious. I suspect that if *The Dictator Pope* had carried the author's real name from the beginning, it would have sold even better.

Pseudonyms never seem to increase sales. That isn't their purpose. Their purpose is to hide authors' identities. If an author has any name recognition at all, then the use of a pseudonym probably depresses sales. He loses out on selling to people who might have purchased the book purely on the strength of his name but otherwise would not have done so, and the use of a pseudonym—at least an obvious one, such as "Marcantonio Colonna"—suggests to many people that the writer may be ashamed of something he has written and doesn't want to be associated with it, perhaps because it is written poorly, perhaps because it is written untruthfully. Neither perception prompts sales. Nevertheless, as I noted, *The Dictator Pope* sold well and ranked for weeks at the top of categories that have a lot of competition, much of it from accomplished writers.

Asked about his use of a pseudonym, Colonna said, "Sadly, what emerges in the book is Pope Francis's tendency to vindictiveness. The present-day curia lives in a state of fear that any criticism of the pope will lead to dismissal, as it did in the case of three officials of the Congregation for the Doctrine of the Faith who were summarily dismissed by Francis without explanation. Those who wish to tell the truth are therefore compelled to anonymity, to protect not only themselves but those around them."

In an email exchange with the *Catholic Herald*, a British publication, Colonna was "asked whether he thought his anonymity would last." He replied: "Under the present pope, the Vatican machine has taken espionage to a new level, and I have little doubt that they will unmask me eventually, perhaps after a few more false casts. But they will need to ask themselves whether it is at the cost of giving me more publicity."

As it turned out, Colonna's new publisher revealed his true identity. In February 2018 Regnery Publishing said it would bring out a print edition of Colonna's book, somewhat revised, in April, and before its publication the author's real name would be announced. The actual announcement came neither from the Vatican, at the conclusion of an investigation, nor from Regnery but via the Knights of Malta, who issued a press release that said Henry Sire had been kicked out of the order for having criticized the pope so vociferously.

\* \* \*

*The Remnant* is a biweekly newspaper that styles itself the chief organ of English-language Catholic Traditionalism. Founded in 1968, it has become an apologist for the Society of St. Pius X, the religious order founded by Archbishop Marcel Lefebvre. (Years ago, *The Remnant* was standoffish regarding the SSPX, but, like a candidate who at last wins election, the publication has "grown in office.") Many of its contributors are little known even within Traditionalist circles. One such is Jason Morgan, who teaches at a university in Chiba, Japan. In an article about the Vatican's changing relationship with China,[13] he has this paragraph:

> And who is this "dictator pope," what does he want? It should be clear by now that Bergoglio is an arch Modernist, that is to say, a heresiarch who seems to hold no Catholic dogma sacred. To Francis, everything is fair game. He upends everything, glibly remarking that "time is bigger than space." (Translation: I will make the mess, but somebody else will have to clean it up.) But Francis is not a bull in a china shop; he is a sniper with a powerful scope. One by one, he is picking off his targets. Traditional marriage, blasted away with a tiny footnote in a poorly-written document. Unmistakable teaching against sodomy, laid low by five little words uttered seemingly absent-mindedly on an airplane. The

Council of Trent, murdered by a postage stamp. Even hell, it now seems, has been shot out of the dogmatic picture. The list goes on and on and on. Francis is not a buffoon pottering about, breaking things in the chapel. He is systematically destroying whatever is left of the Church that Christ founded. He is, in a word, Modernism exemplified.

Let's parse this.

1. Morgan takes it as a given—he makes no attempt at proof—that the pope is a Modernist and a heresiarch (not just a heretic but a super-heretic, at the level of Martin Luther or Arius).

2. The pope is so far gone that he seemingly "hold[s] no Catholic dogma sacred." Not one? He doesn't believe in the Incarnation, the Virgin Birth, the Resurrection, the Real Presence, the Trinity? This would mean that José Bergoglio not only isn't pope, but he isn't even a Christian.

3. Francis "blasted away" marriage. Likewise with the teaching against sodomy. Likewise with the Council of Trent, which was done in by putting Luther's visage on a Vatican postage stamp. (How little it takes to upend an ecumenical council!) Francis even disbelieves in hell; here Morgan gives more weight to the representations of an atheist interviewer who took no notes than to Francis's many hellfire-and-brimstone statements in other contexts.

4. None of this disarray has occurred by inadvertence. "Francis is not a buffoon." No, "he is systematically destroying whatever is left of the Church that Christ founded."

What is curious about this article—which ostensibly is about relations with China—is that it is followed by no corrections or reservations from the editor or chief writers of *The Remnant*. Its publication suggests that they think Morgan has not overstated his case. If, in their own writings, they have been more judicious in their claims, nevertheless they have made room for conclusions that others have drawn (such as that Francis is not a valid pope at all) but they have not yet stated, though those conclusions seem to be logical consequences of what they have permitted to see published.

I do not wish to belabor what likely is obvious to many observers: that there is within Catholic Traditionalism a segment—whether proportionately large or small is hard to say—that is incapable of looking at the pope at arm's length. These commentators are disinclined (or perhaps unable) to make the sorts of distinctions found throughout the three chief books discussed in these pages, *The Dictator Pope*, *Lost Shepherd*, and *To Change the Church*. Of the three, the first is the most tendentious, and, as I noted, it has substantial evidentiary problems, but even it is remarkably different in tone from what various people have written at *The Remnant*, and this is so even though the author of *The Dictator Pope* is himself a Traditionalist.

* * *

At his blog, akaCatholic, Louie Verrecchio says, "For years, I was warmly welcomed as a presenter in Catholic parishes and dioceses throughout the United States, primarily on the topic of Vatican Council II—delivering talks at large archdiocesan conferences, parish level events, and at workshops designed specifically for deacons and directors of religious education. My writing was disseminated via several Catholic media outlets, both diocesan and private. I was a frequently invited 'guest expert' on conservative Catholic radio networks and even made an appearance on EWTN."

In 2004 Verrecchio published *Harvesting the Fruit of Vatican II Faith Formation Series*, which received an imprimatur from a bishop and endorsements from prominent Catholics, among them Cardinal George Pell, Fr. Peter M. J. Stravinskas, and columnist Russell Shaw. Within a decade Verrecchio disavowed that book and his work defending Vatican II. On becoming a Traditionalist, he concluded that the documents of Vatican II "are polluted with ambiguities, contradictions, and outright errors: like an entire lump spoiled by a little leaven, the text of Vatican II, far from being solid nourishment for the soul, is downright poisonous."[14]

Verrecchio says that his current mission "is to examine every proposition that claims to be 'Catholic' through the lens of tradition—regardless of the source, and to scrutinize all things in the light of that which comes to us from God through Holy Mother Church. Doing so in our day necessarily means making powerful enemies, some of whom (with pectoral cross, crozier, and mitre) will even go so far as to use their influence to prevent people like me from earning an honest living. If such is my punishment for the crime of criticizing not only the council but also the all-too-often heterodox words and deeds of the popes, the bishops, and others—so be it."

Verrecchio has become more than a critic of an ecumenical council. A few years ago he came out against the Ordinary Form: "The new Mass, just as Cardinal [Alfredo] Ottaviani [1890-1979] warned in his famous Intervention, leads to a loss of Catholic faith, if not for all who frequent the rite (save only for those spared by the grace of God), for many if not most who do so."[15] Verrecchio advises against attending an Ordinary Form Mass even to fulfill a Sunday obligation.

He has become a particularly bitter foe of Pope Francis, far more bitter than most other Traditionalist commentators. His is perhaps a singular case. I know of no other public proponent of Vatican II who, almost overnight, became a public opponent. His transmogrification has been swift, accomplished in less than five years. He has gone from being a popular speaker at parishes throughout the country, explaining and defending the council, to someone who now speaks infrequently in public venues but writes heatedly against positions he held not long ago. From time to time he refers to his financial straits, going so far as to say at one point that he was thinking about closing down his blog since it was not providing him with even a basic income.

Of the people quoted in this book, Verrecchio likely is furthest removed from a run-of-the-mill conservative religious posture. He is included here as an example of a *type*, the ideologue who has taken his principles to their logical conclusion. To outside observers he might be considered something of a madman, in G. K. Chesterton's sense: "The madman is not the man who has lost his reason. The madman is the man who has lost everything except his reason."[16] Verrecchio is a reasonable man, but his reason takes him down convoluted paths into shadows, not into light.

He reminds me of one-time Catholic apologist Gerry Matatics, who, a few years after converting from Presbyterianism to Catholicism, "converted" once more but to Traditionalist Catholicism. Unable to find surcease there, he kept "converting," and within a decade of his entering the Catholic Church he had become a sedevacantist, at least *in petto* if not in public. (He realized that if he admitted his sympathies his speaking engagements, almost all of which were at "Novus Ordo parishes," would dry up, as would his income. As it happened, they did, and it did, regardless.)

Matatics, like Verrecchio, kept "converting." He wasn't content with attending the Latin Mass. He developed a critique of the English-language Mass. He knew enough Latin to know that "for all" was not a pristine translation of "*pro multis*," which is more accurately rendered as "for many," but his grasp of sacramental theology was not as strong as his grasp of Latin, and he concluded—with others before him—that the new translation resulted in a failed Consecration, at least of the wine, at what is now termed the Ordinary Form Mass. Once Matatics settled on that insight, other things inevitably followed. As Lenin was fond of saying, "Who says A must say B." If the Consecration of the wine fails, so must the Consecration of the bread. If the double Consecration fails, the Mass fails. The post-Vatican II form of the Mass thus had to be defective at its core and no Mass at all.

If that was so, then what about the other sacraments that were revised after the council? What about the council itself? How could the other sacraments remain valid if the key sacrament, the Eucharist, had been rendered void? And how could any of that happen except if Vatican II itself had been a usurpation? And who did the usurping? It must have been the wayward bishops who attended the council, since they approved its sixteen documents, with near unanimity in most cases. How could they all have been taken in by the relatively few bishops who, forming a cabal, steered the council in the direction of their choosing? There must have been a mass apostasy of the world's bishops—even though most of them had been consecrated by such orthodox popes as Pius XII and Pius XI, the "liberal" John XXIII having named only a small proportion of the total episcopate.

For Matatics the result of his relentless logic was the realization that there may be no validly-ordained priests left in the world—or at least none that can be identified with sufficient certainty or that live within reasonable range. Even those breakaway bishops, illicitly ordained, who celebrated the Old Mass were suspect, if for no other reason than that they mentioned the name of the reigning pontiff at the prescribed place in the liturgy. That was enough to show dereliction, and possibly apostasy, on their part. In the end, there was nothing to do but to adopt a "home alone" approach, and that is what the Matatics family did. Its members no longer attended Mass—everything nearby labeled a Mass was nothing more than a simulacrum—but stayed home on Sunday mornings to recite the rosary together and the listen attentively as the *pater familias* led them in prayer.

It should have been little wonder, then, that when one of Matatics's sons married in 2015, the wedding was held not in a church before a priest but in a hotel room where Matatics himself led the ceremony. Such is the iron logic of a man who is all logic. As Chesterton said of the super-logical madman, "Perhaps the nearest we can get to expressing it is to say this: that his mind moves in a perfect but narrow circle. A small circle is quite as infinite as a large circle; but, though it is quite as infinite, it is not so large."[17]

Louie Verrecchio hasn't gone as far as Gerry Matatics. He hasn't adopted the "home alone" position, though he has rejected Vatican II and all its pomps, but his transition has been swifter than Matatics's. That said, there is no indication that his journey has reached a resting point, let alone a settled end point.

Consider a blog post in which Verrecchio restated his thinking regarding Pope Francis, among much else:

Setting aside entirely valid questions (which I've addressed many times in this space) about the so-called resignation of Benedict XVI, its validity, and thus the validity of the conclave that followed,

Francis is utterly unique with respect to the faithful's ability to recognize him as a formal, notorious, pertinacious heretic. There is no question in my mind whatsoever that he is precisely this—a formal, notorious, pertinacious heretic; a man who has severed his relationship with the Mystical Body of Christ—and such a one simply cannot be the head of said Body. The uniqueness of Francis among the post-conciliar claimants to the papacy lies not so much in the plainness of his heresies and the unprecedented boldness with which he promotes them, but rather in the way in which he has been formally warned, admonished, and corrected.[18]

Here Verrecchio positions himself as a limited-application sedevacantist. Most sedevacantists claim that there has been no valid pope since the death of Pius XII in 1958. The conclave that elected John XXIII was comprised of cardinals all of whom had been appointed by Pius XII or by his predecessor, Pius XI. Both were indisputably orthodox men of conservative temperament. It would be difficult to argue that more than a token number of cardinals present at the 1958 conclave could be labeled, legitimately, as theological liberals. (There certainly were theologically liberal bishops at Vatican II, but neither of the Piuses was inclined to raise to the cardinalate men of liberal persuasions.) This means it is more than highly unlikely—it is nearly inconceivable—that the 1958 conclave was steered by a liberal cabal that orchestrated the election of a man not otherwise qualified to be elected.

Despite all this, most sedevacantists claim that John XXIII was not a true pope. Their argument becomes a little easier for them at the time of John's death in 1963: they claim that Vatican II, then in progress, was an illegitimate council promoting false teachings and that any bishops present at the council who voted for its decrees forfeited their right to be called orthodox. This included the cardinals of that time and thereafter, which meant that subsequent papal elections failed because heretics were electing heretics.

The sedevacantist argument makes no sense, and it is not my purpose to grapple with it here. I wish to note only that there is a kind of logic to it: a long string of anti-popes as a consequence of heretical thinking on their part and on the part of the cardinals who voted for them.

Louie Verrecchio distinguishes himself from these sedevacantists by claiming only that Francis is an illegitimate pope. His predecessors going back to John XXIII, however misguided they may have been, seem to have been legitimate, if deeply flawed, popes in his eyes. What chiefly distinguishes Francis from his several immediate predecessors is public correction. Referring to Francis's predecessors, Verrecchio says, "[N]ot one of them in my view was publicly, solemnly, and formally warned, admonished, and corrected in a manner sufficient to condemn themselves as formal, notorious, pertinacious heretics." In his mind, a pope might in fact be a heretic, but until there is a public and formal correction (by whom?), he doesn't cross the line and become a notorious and pertinacious heretic. But if *that* happens, then he ceases to qualify to hold the papal office, and he becomes an anti-pope. That's the status Francis now has, says Verrecchio.

To prove his contention, Verrecchio quotes a priest-theologian, Pietro Ballerini (1698-1769), who said that an erring pope could be corrected publicly by the cardinals, the Roman clergy, or a synod. That would make the pope's positions public. If he then refused to set aside his heterodox teachings, then "in a certain way he had abdicated the pontificate." Verrecchio goes further and asserts that the public correction of a pope can be done by laymen too. He doesn't say how many lay complainants there would need to be to un-pope a pope. But no matter. "Even if the cardinals and bishops (or a portion thereof) never get around to doing their duty, the plain observable fact that Francis has already condemned himself and has separated himself from the Body of the Church remains unchanged, and there is no reason for those with eyes to see to pretend otherwise."

In other words, Verrecchio holds that Francis is an anti-pope and thus no pope at all, no matter his place of residence, his title, his clothing, or the obeisance given to him by Vatican functionaries.

Verrecchio seems to be a conflicted man. At least in theological terms—or, more precisely, in ecclesiological terms—his friends of a decade ago, when he was touring the country promoting Vatican II—might wonder what got into him. I insert mention of him here because he is a

THE ANONYMOUS COMPLAINANT

good bad example. He is an articulate and sometimes even witty castigator of Francis. There are others in the Traditionalist wing whose opinions mirror his, but almost to a man (and they almost all seem to be men, at least those who are active online) their invective is not as sprightly or their heat as intense.

Verrecchio writes like a man betrayed. He had devoted years to defending a sham council. He has seen the light but is resentful of having been so long in the dark. His mode of argumentation is not unlike that of a few other Traditionalist writers, but his is a purer fire. Perhaps it is a consequence of greater natural talents. He had what seems to have been a fairly successful career as a defender of Vatican II. While he made no fortune from his work, he made a living, and that suggests abilities that are uncommon: speaking skills, writing skills, interpersonal skills.

We now know beyond any shadow of any doubt whatsoever that Francis is someone who, to be as charitable as possible, cannot be trusted to tell the truth.

*Amoris Laetitia* was never meant as mere material for "reflection." Its primary purpose is precisely about Communion for the divorced and "remarried," just as the footnote that Francis claimed not to remember makes plain. In fact, according to Francis himself, "there are no other interpretations" of that dreadful document, and what's more, he doesn't just want people "reflecting and dialoguing" about it; rather, he wants it to be considered "authentic magisterium."

The author of *The Dictator Pope*, in my view, succeeded in defending his thesis; namely, that Francis is a "dictator who rules by fear." The point that he misses, however, is that Francis is far more dangerous than this. Pure dictators are not simply feared by their underlings; they are despised by the overwhelming majority of their subjects. In the case of Francis, things are very different.

While dictators often employ propaganda to appear as something other than what they are, no one buys it, most especially outsiders. Francis, by contrast, has somehow managed to fool a great number of Catholics and non-Catholics alike into believing that he really is God's "humble" gift to the Church. An even greater feat (and danger), in my opinion, is that he has also managed to convince far more persons still—including no small number of self-identified Traditionalists—that he's actually Catholic!

Long story short, while *The Dictator Pope* is a decent enough read to recommend, it doesn't address the actual problem. Jorge Bergoglio isn't so much a "dictator pope" who is failing to reform the Roman curia; he is a heretic posing as a pope who is succeeding, humanly speaking, in destroying the Church, dragging countless souls to hell in the process.

The one persistent note in Louie Verrecchio's writing on Pope Francis is that of bitterness. Bitterness colors everything he writes about the pope, and it is an interesting, if discouraging, exercise to examine the changing tone of Verrecchio's blog posts over the last few years as they moved from disagreement to hostility and from hostility to repugnance.

He seems to enjoy adolescent mockery, evinced particularly in the way he titles his blog posts. In a five-week period he published three particularly tendentious pieces about Pope Francis. (These were not his only anti-Francis pieces, though.) One blog post was titled "The Latest Stunt from the Bergoglian Circus."[19] Referring to a papal press conference on board an airplane, the text began this way: "The Greatest Show 30,000 Feet Above Earth, otherwise known as the Bergoglian Circus, is in the news once again."

The title for a post about a papal address to curial officials was "Message to Roman Curia: Big Humble is Watching."[20]

Another post featured a rhetorical question as its headline, with a clear implication of how the reader should answer the question: "Is Bergoglio 'under the Control of Satan'?"[21] (Hedging his bets only slightly, in the text of the post Verrecchio said, "[T]here can be no doubt whatsoever that Francis is—if not under the control of Satan—the Evil One's most powerful servant alive and active in the world today." It isn't clear how Satan's "most powerful servant" couldn't be under his control—if he isn't, who could be?)

As impolitic and impolite as Verrecchio's blog posts tend to be, he usually comes off as a gentleman compared to many of those who comment on his posts. Almost all of the commenters use "handles" or pseudonyms. Few use what appear to be their real names. This is understandable, since they likely believe, at least subconsciously, that if their remarks could be attributed to them they would lose face and probably friends, not just on Facebook but at home and in the work place.

An anonymous commenter to the post titled "The Latest Stunt from the Bergoglian Circus" had this to say: "Yes, [Pope Francis] becomes more obvious in his heresies every day. Why? Because absolutely no one is going to stop him. What will be God's response when the silent cardinals, bishops, and priests face their final judgment? The only explanation is that many/most/all of them do not believe they will face a final judgment in the first place. Godless apostates."

Another commenter—again anonymous (that is, using a "handle" to disguise his identity)—added this: "I know, you say he's not pope. I say he's a Judas pope. Such is consistent with the mystery of iniquity and the messiness it produces in this world. We see through a glass but darkly. What's clear though is that this Francis character—pope or not—is making a mess just as he vowed to do."

A third commenter added these remarks: "When the visible head (the pope) is not in conformity with the

Invisible Head (Christ), he loses all authority and must be resisted. Am I understanding this incorrectly? If so, Bergoglio must be resisted because he has proven to be an enemy of Christ and his Church whether he is legitimate or not."

These are representative comments that follow the post about the "Bergoglian Circus." They are representative not only of the other posts in that thread but of posts in other threads at Verrecchio's website. He does nothing to correct or admonish these commenters or any others. His absence from the comment stream could be interpreted more than one way. Perhaps he doesn't have time to police what his followers say. Perhaps he largely disagrees with them but holds back from criticizing them because he wants a freewheeling discussion, one that might tend to draw additional visitors. Or perhaps he doesn't much disagree with what commenters such as the ones quoted above say. He could be using them to put into words more extreme thoughts that he is unwilling, for whatever reason, to put his own name to.

Verrecchio likely would like to have additional visitations to his website. Over a recent 30-day period he drew 71,900 visits.[22] It's important here to distinguish visits from unique visitors. If each person who visited Verrecchio's website during that period visited ten times, then the total number of unique visitors would have been 7,190. As a comparison, the Traditionalist-leaning LifeSite News website receive 618,600 unique visits during the same 30-day period[23]—that's unique visitors as distinguished from Verrecchio's total visits. This means that LifeSite News might be generating as much as 100 times as much traffic as Verrecchio's website. Granted, LifeSite News is a comparably large operation, with a full complement of employees, while Verrecchio works as a sole proprietor. The point remains: he likely would welcome more traffic because traffic can be transformed into income, and Verrecchio several times has noted his outfit's thin budget. He has appealed for financial help and has said that if things did not turn around that he would have to consider altering or ending his online work.

So, part of Verrecchio's reluctance to chastise commenters who write especially egregious things may be financial: he may think that by letting them have elbow room he might attract additional like-minded people, but he must realize that such an approach could result in fewer, not more, regular visitors, if people who drop by are turned off by a plethora of off-the-wall comments.

This leads me to think he leaves up the particularly wild comments—which usually form a majority of the comments to any one post—because he largely agrees with them. He sees them as echoing his own thoughts, even unexpressed ones. Perhaps some of them will prove to foreshadow his future writings. However that turns out, his website serves as a good reminder of what happens when free rein is given to people whose intemperance is magnified by their anonymity. It is one thing to criticize a pope on a matter here or a matter there. It is something else to go after a pope with an intensity not normally seen outside the anti-Catholicism of certain Protestant sectarians of yesteryear.

# Chapter 2

# The Avuncular Scold

The second major book to consider Pope Francis from a conservative Catholic perspective was Philip F. Lawler's *Lost Shepherd*,[24] which was published in February 2018. First, though, something about Lawler.

A native of the Boston area, Lawler attended Harvard, where he graduated with honors while majoring in government. Later he attended the University of Chicago before entering journalism. In 1996 he founded Catholic World News, which he says was "the first English-language Catholic news service operating on the Internet."[25] He has been its editor ever since. CWN was acquired by the non-profit Trinity Communications in 2006, and the news service appears at the Catholic Culture website.[26] Trinity Communications was established in 1985 by Jeffrey Mirus, who formerly taught at Christendom College, which he co-founded with several other Catholic laymen. Today he and Lawler are the chief writers for CWN.

Lawler has worked in multiple editorial capacities and for various organizations. At the Heritage Foundation he was managing editor of *Policy Review*. Later he was an editor at *Crisis* magazine and then was the chief editor at *Catholic World Report*, which is published by Ignatius Press.

For many years Lawler was active in conservative politics, largely as an organizer and speechwriter for candidates at local, state, and national levels but also as a candidate himself. In 2000 he ran for U.S. Senate against Edward Kennedy. (Lawler lost.)

Aside from *Lost Shepherd*, Lawler has written five books, the best known being *The Faithful Departed: The Collapse of Boston's Catholic Culture* (2010), which traced "the rise and fall of the Catholic Church as a cultural dynamo in Boston, showing how the Massachusetts experience set a pattern that has echoed throughout the United States as religious institutions have lost social influence in the face of rising secularization."[27]

Lawler's wife, Leila, runs a blog for young mothers (where she is known as "Auntie Leila") and has been active online in discussions regarding the pope. For his part, Phil Lawler describes himself as a "beekeeper, tennis player, music lover, cross-country skier, [and] Red Sox fan," the last item not being something that should be held against him.

In the following pages I present extracts from *Lost Shepherd*, to give a sense of Lawler's tone and approach. The extracts come from the first thirty and the final forty pages of the book. Before presenting them I should note, in the interest of full disclosure, that the back cover of the book includes an endorsement from me:

After giving Pope Francis every benefit of the doubt, Philip Lawler reluctantly concluded that there were serious problems with this papacy. A conscientious and well-connected writer, Lawler explains without exaggeration or histrionics why we must hope for a successor who can right the Barque of Peter quickly, before too many passengers lose hope or abandon ship.

That was my evaluation after receiving a pre-publication copy of the text and reading it slowly and thoroughly. I make a point of saying "slowly and thoroughly" because many critics of the book seem to have read it—if they read it at all—hastily and without due seriousness, affecting to know (or imagining to know) what Lawler meant to say, even if he never quite said what they accused him of saying.

The discerning reader will see at once that I thought the book to be judicious and largely in conformity with my own thoughts about recent events in the Church. This doesn't mean that I agreed with everything Lawler said or with each of his emphases, but then I suppose I never have agreed completely with any book that was non-inspired (just as probably no readers of my books ever have agreed with everything I said in them—even though they should have).

As will become evident later, I think some critics of *Lost Shepherd* have misconstrued its argument or have seen in it things that just aren't there. Although not as dispassionately written as Ross Douthat's later-appearing *To Change the*

*Church*, Lawler's book isn't tendentious the way Henry Sire's *The Dictator Pope* is. Like Douthat, but unlike Sire, Lawler puts some of himself into his book, and he does so particularly at the beginning, which is where we will begin the extracts. Here are the opening paragraphs from the introduction.

> Every day I pray for Pope Francis. And every day (I am exaggerating, but only slightly), the pope issues another reminder that he does not approve of Catholics like me.

> If the Holy Father were rebuking me for my sins, I would have no reason to complain. But day after weary day, in his homilies at morning Mass in the Vatican's St. Martha residence, the pope upbraids me—and countless thousands of other faithful Catholics—for clinging to, and sometimes suffering for, the truths that the Church has always taught. We are rigid, he tells us. We are the "doctors of the law," the Pharisees, who only want to be "comfortable" with our Faith.

> In the early days of his pontificate, Francis captured the public imagination with his call for a new, vigorous, worldwide mission. I was one of millions caught up in the "Francis effect," enthusiastic about his vision. I found that friends and neighbors, inspired by what they read and heard about the pope,

wanted to talk with me about the Catholic Faith: not about the politics of the Vatican or the scandals of the clergy, but about the fundamental message of the gospel.

As time passed, however, the tone and even the content of the pope's public statements puzzled me, then distressed me. For months in my work reporting on the daily news from the Vatican, I did my best to provide reassurance—for my readers and sometimes for myself—that despite his sometimes alarming remarks, Francis was not a radical, was not leading the Church away from the ancient sources of the Faith. But gradually, reluctantly, painfully, I came to the conclusion that he was.

The Roman pontiff should be a focus of unity in the Church. Francis, regrettably, has become a source of division. There are two reasons for this unhappy development: the pope's autocratic style of governance and the radical nature of the program that he is relentlessly advancing.[28]

Like many other Catholics, Lawler was "caught up in the 'Francis effect.'" He saw that people around him, Catholics and non-Catholics alike, perked their ears at the mention of the new pope. They wanted to talk about things Catholic, many for the first time. There was something in the air and something on the airwaves.

That sense of fresh beginnings has lasted to this day for many people, but Lawler had a seat that most people never occupy, that of a journalist looking in detail at each day's Vatican news. And he had contacts, there and elsewhere, available to few. He learned about things that most people, even those interested in religious topics, just don't learn about, and he began to get a different sense of Francis. But that was the added stuff. There was enough public stuff, which was available to everyone. "[T]he pope's public statements puzzled me, then distressed me."

Let's pause here. That sentence could have been written by countless people, including many who exulted when they saw Cardinal Jorge Bergoglio emerge on St. Peter's balcony as Pope Francis. I have come across not a few defenders of the pope who cheekily claim that no one—no one at all—has been puzzled or distressed by Francis. This has struck me as an unreasonable if understandable defensive tack. Those making the claim might feel no puzzlement or distress. In their regard for the institution of the papacy they have projected their own sanguinity onto the generality of believers. But the refutation of their claim is simple and obvious: there are lots of people who say they are puzzled or distressed. It is as though an art critic claims that everyone likes the work of Jackson Pollock, but his claim is refuted definitively by noting that many people say they don't care for Pollock's work at all.

Let me skip to Lawler's final paragraph above. He says that the pope—any pope—should be a "focus of unity in the Church." This is precisely Christ's will for the papacy:

"I have prayed for you that your faith may not fail; and when you have turned again, strengthen your brethren" (Luke 22:32). Lawler has concluded that Francis "has become a source of division." This conclusion may be taken either as incontestable or as dependent. It is incontestable if Lawler means that the current papacy has become caught up in division in a way unknown in recent times. That books such as *The Dictator Pope*, *Lost Shepherd*, and *To Change the Church* have been written at all is conclusive testimony to that.

On the other hand, saying that Francis "has become a source of division" might be interpreted as saying that the divisions that have arising during his papacy are of the pope's making (whether intentionally or unintentionally), rather than being things that have arisen *while* he has been pope but not necessarily *because* he has been pope. Here, I think, there is latitude for disagreement—or at least for nuance and careful delineation of acts and consequences.

Let me return to Lawler's penultimate paragraph above. Here it appears that he has written with less care than might have been warranted. He says he thought that, "despite his sometimes alarming remarks, Francis was not a radical, was not leading the Church away from the ancient sources of the Faith. But gradually, reluctantly, painfully, I came to the conclusion that he was." The unclear part is the sense that Francis has been "leading the Church away from the ancient sources of the Faith."

What Lawler means by this is not clear in this introduction to his book, and it never quite becomes resolved in the remainder of the book, mainly because the charge is indeterminate in content and time. One reader might read it narrowly, as referring to the issue of Communion for the divorced and remarried but not much beyond that. Another might read it broadly, as saying that Francis is rejecting, wholesale, the ancient patrimony of the Church, such as the teachings of the Fathers of the Church. That is not at all what Lawler claims; it is not what any of the pope's critics have claimed, not even the most febrile. I have yet to come across anyone who thinks that Francis is trying to jettison the Church of the early (and of later) centuries, but I can see how someone might read into Lawler's phrasing ("ancient sources of the Faith") such a massive assertion.

This brings me to the next extract.

> I found I could no longer pretend that Francis was merely offering a novel interpretation of Catholic doctrine. No, it was more than that. He was engaged in a deliberate effort to change what the Church teaches.[29]

Here again there is imprecision. It is one that Lawler clears up later in the book. There is a distinction between a pope trying to alter formal Church teaching—imagine him trying to drop a line or two from the Nicene Creed or trying to insert their opposites—and his allowing some teaching to slide into abeyance, either through non-enforcement or silence. The practical result, for the man in the pew, might be nearly the same, but there is a distinction nevertheless.

Recognizing the problem can also provide a sort of relief, a relaxation of accumulating tensions. When I tell friends that I consider this papacy a disaster, more often than not they feel oddly reassured. They can relax a bit, knowing that their own misgivings are not irrational, that others share their fears about the future of the Faith, that they need not continue a fruitless search for ways to reconcile the irreconcilable.

Moreover, having given the problem a proper name, they can recognize what this crisis of Catholicism is not and put aside the explanations offered by some radical Traditionalists. Francis is not an anti-pope, much less the Antichrist. The See of Peter is not vacant, and Benedict is not the "real" pontiff.[30]

Writing online in response to comments critical of *Lost Shepherd*, Lawler and his wife have used "disaster" to refer to the current papacy, and Leila has written that she and Phil consider Francis to be a "bad pope." Elsewhere I will look at that term and its historical connections, but I want to note here that the Lawlers have fixed on terms that in part must be reflective of the disappointment that Phil Lawler expressed as early as the second paragraph of his book. Sometimes disappointment can lead one to use a term that can be interpreted by others too variously for convenience. "Disaster" seems to be such a term.

Some will take it narrowly. As mentioned above, they may think only in terms of what they perceive to be the pastoral consequences of a few words in *Amoris Laetitia*. They may extrapolate what they think will happen to those people, whether few or many, who begin to present themselves for Communion when, under a prior understanding, they had no right to do so.

Others will take "disaster" in a broader sense, as though applying to many or most aspects of Francis's papacy, not just to the effects of a single apostolic exhortation but to effects arising from his managerial or administrative style and actions. Instead of having one thing to gripe about they have scores, at which point the whole of Francis' papacy seems to be under a cloud.

> Francis had developed an odd style, emerging as a scold. His rhetoric was radically at odds with his public statements about the need to "accompany" sinners, to tolerate disagreements, to reach out to new constituencies. In his own preaching he hectored his listeners, denouncing more than encouraging.[31]

That sentence encapsulates Francis's consistent advice to Church leaders: a plea for compassion, tolerance, willingness to listen, and reluctance to pass judgment. And the popular perception is that the pope is just that sort of prelate: kind, soft-spoken, avuncular, uniting rather than dividing. Yet even a cursory reading of the pope's daily homilies reveals harsh rhetoric, stinging rebukes, and angry denunciations such as we have not heard from a Roman pontiff for generations.[32]

These two paragraphs, which appear on sequential pages near the end of *Lost Shepherd*, point to things that some of the pope's defenders skip over almost entirely. Online apologists Dave Armstrong and Pete Vere, for example, have had little to say about the pope's rhetoric, which not infrequently verges on the rude. Their writings in his defense have been almost exclusively about doctrinal matters. They have argued that, contrary to reports in unreliable popular media, Francis has not denied Catholic doctrines (such as his supposed rejection of the existence of hell), but they have given scant attention to the pope's bureaucratic or organizational actions. Back to Lawler.

> Whether it is an odd administrative style or a quirk of personality that makes Francis so hard on his critics, it cannot be denied that he is loyal to his allies. In fact, it has become apparent that this pope selects his associates on the basis of personal loyalty rather than theological acumen or pastoral performance. Among the prelates he has chosen as his closest advisers, several have displayed characteristics that he has roundly denounced in his public statements.

> Take for instance the leaders of the Council of Cardinals, which he established to advise him on Vatican reforms. The man appointed coordinator of this influential group is the Honduran cardinal Oscar Rodríguez Maradiaga, who once dismissed sex-abuse complaints against the clergy as a creation of the

American media—which, he observed, were disproportionately controlled by Jewish interests. (He later apologized for that remark.)[33]

Nearly any pope, I suppose, "selects his associates on the basis of personal loyalty," at least to some extent, but he also tries to select men with "theological acumen or pastoral performance." Lawler thinks Francis has been something of an exception, and later in his book he gives examples beyond that of Cardinal Rodríguez Maradiaga.

Even after his rude dismissal, [Cardinal Gerhard] Müller continued to defend the pope, insisting— against all evidence—that his departure was a matter of administrative routine rather than ideological incompatibility. "There were no differences between me and Pope Francis," he told the *Allgemeine Zeitung* of Mainz. The pontiff had decided to end the practice of routinely extending Vatican appointments, he said, and "I happened to be the first one to which this applied." (Three other prominent Vatican officials had completed their five-year appointments in the past few months, and all three had remained in place.)

A few days later, however, still proclaiming that he was "always loyal to the pope and always will be," Müller did criticize the shabby way he had been treated: "I cannot accept this way of doing things."

Recalling Francis's earlier firings of clerics on the CDF staff, Müller said that Church leaders should be bound by the precepts of Catholic social teaching in treating their employees with dignity.[34]

Prefects of Vatican dicasteries commonly are appointed for five-year terms, and commonly their terms are renewed at least once. Joseph Ratzinger, the future Benedict XVI, served as prefect of the Congregation for the Doctrine of the Faith (Müller was his second successor, after the American William Levada) from 1981 until his election as pope in 2005, which means his five-year term was renewed four times. When Müller's first and only term was nearing its end in 2017, he received no communication from Francis about a possible renewal. Customarily notice of renewal or non-renewal is made months in advance, so the prefect can make appropriate arrangements. It was only on the very last day of his term that Müller was informed that there would be no renewal.

I have yet to find a defender of the pope who has addressed this incident. It could not have been a matter of mere oversight, of forgetfulness or an overlooked item on a to-do list. If it had been, the prefect would have received a note of apology for the faux pas. It is difficult to see how what occurred could be interpreted as anything but a deliberate slight, and that is how Müller took it: "I cannot accept this way of doing things." As Lawler characterized it, it was a "rude dismissal." One struggles to think of another modern pope who did anything analogous.

With his words and actions, Francis has devalued the work of his predecessors and thus diminished the teaching office of the papacy. If a Catholic today is free to ignore the teachings of John Paul II, as Francis implies, then a Catholic tomorrow will be free to ignore the teachings of Francis. The only escape from this dilemma is the one suggested by Benedict XVI: the hermeneutic of continuity. Papal teachings must be interpreted, and a pope's pastoral initiatives should be judged, in continuity with two thousand years of Catholic tradition. By that standard, the papacy of Francis has been a disaster for the Church.[35]

Here Lawler again uses "disaster"—but this time with more precision. He and others discussed in this book I have characterized as "conservative Catholics," often enough in the political sense, I suppose, but chiefly in the religious sense as those who emphasize the conservation of Catholic teaching and practice, not just as a preference but as a necessity. If the Catholic Church somehow came to alter its teachings the way some people alter their wardrobes, it might continue as an institution, but it would be an institution without a soul, and it would not be able to continue indefinitely.

If Pope Francis really is trying to set aside the "hermeneutic of continuity" in preference for novelty, if he is trying to work around "two thousand years of Catholic tradition," if he "has devalued the work of his predecessors and thus diminished the teaching office of the papacy," then it might be legitimate to say that the result will be "a disaster for the Church," though even then one should keep in mind the protection of the Holy Spirit.

It is a commonplace that multiple popes have joked that the greatest proof of the divine establishment of the Church is the fact that the it has persisted despite the caliber of the men occupying its lofty offices—and even its neighborhood rectories. Any purely human institution would have disappeared from history centuries ago. This is true of the Catholic Church as a whole and of the papacy in particular.

Here let me make an excursus and quote a marvelous but too-little-known reflection by historian Thomas Babington Macaulay (1800-1859). It appeared in a review of Leopold von Ranke's *History of the Popes* that Macaulay wrote in 1840 for the *Edinburgh Review*. Keep in mind that Macaulay was a Protestant who held not a few anti-Catholic prejudices. (I preserve the original spelling and orthography.)

> There is not, and there never was on this earth, a work of human policy so well deserving of examination as the Roman Catholic Church. The history of that Church joins together the two great ages of human civilisation. No other institution is left standing which carries the mind back to the times when the smoke of sacrifice rose from the Pantheon, and when camelopards and tigers bounded in the Flavian amphitheatre.

The proudest royal houses are but of yesterday, when compared with the line of the Supreme Pontiffs. That line we trace back in an unbroken series, from the Pope who crowned Napoleon in the nineteenth century to the Pope who crowned Pepin in the eighth; and far beyond the time of Pepin the august dynasty extends, till it is lost in the twilight of fable. The republic of Venice came next in antiquity. But the republic of Venice was modern when compared with the Papacy; and the republic of Venice is gone, and the Papacy remains.

The Papacy remains, not in decay, not a mere antique, but full of life and youthful vigour. The Catholic Church is still sending forth to the farthest ends of the world missionaries as zealous as those who landed in Kent with Augustin, and still confronting hostile kings with the same spirit with which she confronted Attila. The number of her children is greater than in any former age. Her acquisitions in the New World have more than compensated for what she has lost in the Old.

Her spiritual ascendency extends over the vast countries which lie between the plains of the Missouri and Cape Horn, countries which a century hence, may not improbably contain a population as large as that which now inhabits Europe. The members of her communion are certainly not fewer than a hundred and fifty millions; and it will be difficult to show that all other Christian sects united amount to a hundred and twenty millions.

Nor do we see any sign which indicates that the term of her long dominion is approaching. She saw the commencement of all the governments and of all the ecclesiastical establishments that now exist in the world; and we feel no assurance that she is not destined to see the end of them all. She was great and respected before the Saxon had set foot on Britain, before the Frank had passed the Rhine, when Grecian eloquence still flourished at Antioch, when idols were still worshipped in the temple of Mecca. And she may still exist in undiminished vigour when some traveller from New Zealand shall, in the midst of a vast solitude, take his stand on a broken arch of London Bridge to sketch the ruins of St. Paul's.

Even someone disinclined to approve of Catholic distinctives, such as Macaulay, needs to admit, however reluctantly, that there has been something singular about the Catholic Church. It just won't do to say the papacy has persisted because the office has been filled by a long line of politically clever maneuverers or that the Catholic Church as a whole has persisted because it repeatedly lucked out and adhered to the "winning side" over the course of twenty centuries.

Now let's turn to the final pages of Lawler's book.

But can the pope be wrong? Or more importantly, can the wrong man occupy the chair of Peter? Again, some pious Catholics assume that with the Holy Spirit guiding the Church, it is impossible for a conclave to choose the wrong man. If only that were the case! When Cardinal Joseph Ratzinger was asked in 1990 if the Holy Spirit chooses the Roman pontiff, the future pope responded:

"I would not say so, in the sense that the Holy Spirit picks out the Pope. . . . I would say that the Spirit does not exactly take control of the affair, but rather like a good educator, as it were, leaves us much space, much freedom, without entirely abandoning us. Thus the Spirit's role should be understood in a much more elastic sense, not that he dictates the candidate for whom one must vote. Probably the only assurance he offers is that the thing cannot be totally ruined. There are too many contrary instances of popes the Holy Spirit obviously would not have picked!"[36]

I always have found curious that many Catholics—the majority of practicing ones, I would say—think that the Holy Spirit positively determines the outcome of conclaves, as though his invocation amounted to an urim and thummin. Such a view stumbles when confronted with names such as John XII and Alexander VI, two of the most unsavory occupants of the Holy See. Could the Holy Spirit have insisted that such men be put at the head of the Church—and, if so, to what positive end?

No, Cardinal Ratzinger was right: "the only assurance he offers is that the thing cannot be totally ruined." That is a modest consolation: very bad things can happen but not a complete failure of the Church. In other words, at times the "wrong" man has been elected pope. Lawler thinks this is what happened in 2013. The Holy Spirit was at work in the conclave, but perhaps too few electors interpreted his promptings properly. Many people may disagree with Lawler on many things, but his understanding of the role of the Holy Spirit is correct. Many defenders of Francis misconstrue Church teaching on this point.

Now we come to the final two paragraphs in *Lost Shepherd*.

Pope Francis has not taught heresy, but the confusion he has stirred up has destabilized the universal Church. The faithful have been led to question themselves, their beliefs, their Faith. They look to Rome for guidance and instead find more questions, more confusion.

For thirty-five years, loyal Catholics were accustomed to looking to Rome for guidance, to ease the confusion that arose from uncertain leadership at the local level. Now the situation has been reversed, particularly in the United States. Some American bishops have become bolder in their defenses of orthodoxy, more willing to risk the disapproval of the secular world. Today they need the encouragement of faithful Catholics, as their duty requires them to risk disapproval from Rome.[37]

"Pope Francis has not taught heresy." Here Lawler distinguishes himself from some critics of the pope, particularly Traditionalists associated with *The Remnant* and similar publications and websites, where the charge of "Heretic!" is bandied about freely. There is a distinction to be made between teaching heresy and teaching so indistinctly that other people end up with heresies of their own fashioning. For Lawler the chief problem with this papacy is the confusion it has engendered. When people are confused, they are liable to go every which way—like sheep who have lost their shepherd.

\* \* \*

My first public comment on *Lost Shepherd* came in a Facebook post that I wrote on December 23, 2017. I titled it "Make a Note to Get This Book on Pope Francis."

Philip Lawler, the editor at Catholic World News, has a new book coming out February 26: *Lost Shepherd: How Pope Francis is Misleading His Flock.* In the introduction Lawler says that, over the course of several years, "I did my best to provide assurance—for my readers and sometimes for myself—that despite his sometimes alarming remarks, Francis was not a radical, was not leading the Church away from the ancient sources of the Faith. But gradually, reluctantly, I came to the conclusion that he was."

Unlike some of the most vocal critics of this pope, Lawler took his time and gave him the benefit of every doubt. The result is 256 pages that lay out recent history well, without exaggeration or histrionics and with enough to substantiate Lawler's reluctant conclusions. Toward the end of the introduction he says, "I found I could no longer pretend that Francis was merely offering a novel interpretation of Catholic doctrine. No, it was more than that. He was engaged in a deliberate effort to change what the Church teaches."

Lawler cautions against following the logic of certain Traditionalists who came out against Francis almost before the new pope stepped out on the balcony to give his first greeting. "Francis is not an anti-pope, much less the Antichrist. The See of Peter is not vacant, and Benedict is not the 'real' pontiff." All such notions are nonsense, says Lawler, and not one of them helps to understand the reality of the situation. In fact, they do nothing but obscure.

The middle half of the book concerns the development and meaning of some of Pope Francis's writings. Much space is given to *Amoris Laetitia*. Lawler says it "is not a revolutionary document. It is a subversive one. Francis has not overthrown the traditional teaching of the Church, as many Catholics hoped or feared that he would." The document gives wide pastoral latitude, enough so that, in practice, in certain areas the traditional teaching of the Church can be set aside while not being denied.

To me the most interesting parts of the book concern Francis's background in Argentina, his personal style (peremptory, conniving, sometimes even using low language), and his very "Jesuitical" machinations before and after becoming pope. In these regards he is quite unlike his predecessors—at least unlike all the other popes of my lifetime. Perhaps most noticeably, Francis has been a scold. "His rhetoric was radically at odds with his pulpit statements about the need to 'accompany' sinners, to tolerate disagreements, to reach out to new constituencies," says Lawler. "In his own preaching he hectored his listeners, denouncing more than encouraging."

The result—especially in consequence of preachings and talks he has given to Vatican officials and staff—has been plummeting morale and a not unjustified fear of accusations of disloyalty. Some Vatican staff members, even prominent members of prominent dicasteries, have been removed without a fare-thee-well, without explanation. Apparently phones have been tapped, conversations overheard. The result has been a widespread fear to say anything critical about anything, lest one lose one's job.

It is then not surprising to learn that "the pope selects his associates on the basis of personal loyalty rather than theological acumen or pastoral performance," concludes Lawyer. I can't help thinking that in certain respects Pope Francis is much like President Trump. Each places more emphasis on loyalty than on skill. Each has gone through lots of aides and associates. The turnover rate at the Vatican, as at the White House, has been high.

What about the vaunted "Francis revival" around the world? There hasn't been one, says Lawler. For example, worldwide the number of seminarians was increasing for years, up through 2012. The number has been in decline since then. Ditto for attendance at the pope's Wednesday audiences. At the beginning of his reign it was common to see 40,000 people or more in St. Peter's Square. Now it's not uncommon to see fewer than 15,000. Francis's two immediate predecessors usually spoke to colonnade-to-colonnade audiences, but something has changed. The enthusiasm has waned.

Did the Holy Spirit goof at the conclave? No, as then-Cardinal Ratzinger noted in 1990: "Thus the

Spirit's role should be understood in a much more elastic sense, not that he dictates the candidate for whom one must vote. Probably the only assurance he offers is that the thing cannot be totally ruined."

But "the thing" has been damaged, insists Lawler. "The damage done by Francis cannot be repaired unless it is recognized. Denying problems and papering over the differences only amplifies the confusion." As for the pope's signature piece, Lawler says, "Yes, there are some fine passages in *Amoris Laetitia*. But on the whole it fails as a teaching document because, as the saying goes, what is good is not new, and what is new is not good."

That said, "Pope Francis has not taught heresy, but the confusion he has stirred up has destabilized the universal Church." Lawler thinks it could take a long time for the Church to find its equilibrium again. One hopes not. . . . One way to minimize that is to read Lawler's book and to understand how a conscientious and well-connected writer came to the conclusions he did.

These comments of mine seem to have surprised some of my apologist friends, among them Dave Armstrong and Pete Vere. As will become clear, they evinced disappointment in my general approval of a book that had the cheek to criticize a sitting pope. It was the beginning of a long and spirited exchange of opinions. Before this we seldom had disagreed on any substantial point of theology or ecclesiology, but now a divide appeared. I was on one side of the gap, and they were on the other. Behind me was another gap, one dividing me from the pope's most ardent critics. In the eyes of one group I was temerarious; in the eyes of the other, too conciliatory.

* * *

Dave Armstrong may not be the most influential Catholic apologist in America, but he almost certainly is the most prolific. He has written about fifty books and hundreds of online articles, most of which have appeared at his blog "Biblical Evidence for Catholicism."[38] He has been a full-time apologist since 2001. Formerly a Protestant, he became Catholic in 1991, being received into the Church by the late John A. Hardon, S.J., a well-regarded scholar and writer. Although Armstrong cooperates with other Catholic apologists and their organizations, he has operated solo, which sometimes has proved difficult financially. Several times during his apologetical career he has found it necessary to supplement his income with side jobs, and for a few years running he sought donations from his readers, gathering about $5,000 each time—enough, he said, to make up the shortfall of his modest income.

Most of Armstrong's books have been self-published and have been compilations and extensions of material that has appeared at his blog. With some frequency he bemoans the slow sales of these books. He seems to have done better with books that have been published traditionally. Six have been brought out by Sophia Institute Press, a few more by other traditional publishers. Those books have produced the best cash flow for him.

Armstrong shies away from public speaking, but he has appeared on Catholic radio programs multiple times. He does not participate in apologetics conferences, and he travels infrequently. His excursions from his Detroit-area home are largely limited to family vacations. He repeatedly has said that his skills are with the written, rather than the oral, word.

With the advent of the Francis papacy Armstrong positioned himself as one of the pope's most persistent defenders and explainers. This has been so since the early days of the pontificate, but Armstrong's efforts have heightened in recent months, as books critical of the pope have appeared. He has taken particular exception to one of the new titles, going so far as to say, "I've been the most vocal critic of Phil Lawler's pathetic book *Lost Shepherd*."

That claim is interesting at two levels. It almost certainly is the case that Armstrong has written more against *Lost Shepherd* than has any other Catholic writer. Others have written more thorough reviews of the book, but he has written multiple reviews (or partial reviews) and has written at least dozens, and perhaps hundreds, of online comments about Lawler and his best-selling book.

The other interesting thing about Armstrong's comment is his use of the adjective "pathetic." Although he considers himself an objective observer of things Catholic, priding himself on searching out original sources and tracking down elusive quotations, when defending Francis he commonly has resorted to tossing around labels and even to name calling. The most common epithet has been "pope basher," his term for those who display criticism of Francis. In March 2018 Armstrong defined "bashing" as "a continual preoccupation or obsession with running down the pope and giving him no benefit of the doubt whatever: up to and including much gossipy lying and a wide-eyed, snickering passing-along of unsubstantiated rumors and conspiracy theories."

Such a focused definition would seem to apply only to a small number of people, such as those who revel in venting their spleen in comment boxes. Such people are preoccupied with Francis, giving him "no benefit of the doubt" and passing along "unsubstantiated rumors and conspiracy theories." Such people exist, and Armstrong's label "pope basher," however infelicitous, might be appropriate for them, but he applies the term to just about anyone who criticizes the pope, including not just authors Henry Sire, Phil Lawler, and Ross Douthat but to others who have disagreed with Armstrong online.

It is true that Sire includes in his book one or two "unsubstantiated rumors" (such as that the Vatican, under Francis, sought to give financial aid to the Hillary Clinton campaign), but on the whole not even Sire can be convicted of mainly dealing in rumors, and neither Lawler nor Douthat can be accused of including any rumors at all in their books. The latter two repeatedly make allowances for papal actions they find inexplicable, and none of the three authors promote conspiracy theories. They and many others labeled as "pope bashers" by Armstrong thus seem not to qualify under his own definition.

* * *

Dave Armstrong was the first to write a review of *Lost Shepherd* at Amazon, where he gave the book one star out of five. He was first in line because Phil Lawler sent him a pre-publication copy of the book. Armstrong's review may be the most appropriate place to begin a consideration of his—and like-minded people's—approach to the Francis papacy. He titled his review "Peeling an Onion: Lawler Fails to Prove His Case."

> Phil Lawler was kind enough to send me a review copy of his book. In the introduction he described Pope Francis and his opinions as follows: "leading the Church away from the ancient sources of the Faith . . . radical nature of the program that he is relentlessly advancing . . . encouraged beliefs and practices that are incompatible with the prior teachings of the Church . . . a Roman pontiff who disregarded so easily what the Church has always taught and believed and practiced on such bedrock issues as the nature of marriage and of the Eucharist . . . a danger to the Faith."

These are extraordinary claims that certainly need very strong demonstration. The problem with the book is that the undeniable proof never came. Thus, reading it reminded me of peeling an onion and eventually discovering that it has no core (unlike an apple), or finding a treasure chest that contains nothing.

Lawler in the introduction cites the pope's homily from February 24, 2017 as, in effect, his final straw. He reports that "Something snapped inside me" after reading what he construes as the Holy Father's capitalizing on "one more opportunity to promote his own view on divorce and remarriage." He concluded: "[I]n this case, the pope turned the Gospel reading completely upside-down. . . . I found I could no longer pretend that Francis was merely offering a novel interpretation of Catholic doctrine. No, it was more than that. He was engaged in a deliberate effort to change what the Church teaches."

The homily was one of many of Pope Francis' characteristic condemnations of legalism and "casuistic logic." Jesus and Paul both strongly opposed the same thing. The point he's making is that Jesus didn't approach the question from merely a legal standpoint, which is how his critics were approaching it. They were doing their usual "straining at gnats" routine and missing the "weightier matters" about marriage and divorce. Jesus went much more deeply into the matter, telling them that God only allowed divorce at all because of their hardness of heart. The pope, too, was trying to bring out the deeper meanings of the passage.

If Lawler claims that the pope has now denied the indissolubility of marriage, then his intellectual burden is to find direct passages where the pope did that. But he did no such thing.

Here Armstrong causes misdirection. He says that it is up to Lawler to prove that the pope "has now denied the indissolubility of marriage" and that Lawler has failed to do so. Armstrong says, "I went and did his work for him," and he offers up "four disproofs of [Lawler's] negative assertion," giving citations to articles in four publications.

The problem is that Lawler doesn't claim that Francis denies the indissolubility of marriage. Armstrong misreads him and works up proof against something not asserted. He does something similar with Lawler's criticism of the pope's "Who am I to judge?" comment, made on a flight when returning to Rome from a visit to Brazil. Armstrong offers several citations that demonstrate that Francis isn't "soft on homosexuality," but Lawler's point wasn't that the pope was "soft" but that he was unclear—a fair point, given how many people interpreted the pope to mean that homosexual sexual relations were, if not permissible, at least not condemnable.

Similarly with the interview Francis had with the elderly journalist Eugenio Scalfari, an atheist, in which Scalfari— who admittedly took no notes and reproduced the interview from memory—claimed that Francis said he disbelieves in hell. Lawler doesn't claim that the pope harbors that heresy; he bemoans the confusion coming from Scalfari's sloppy reporting (or imaginative reconstruction) and faults the pope for carelessness in handling such interviews. (As of this writing, there have been five Francis-Scalfari interviews.) Armstrong says that "Lawler doesn't make the slightest effort to do the necessary research" to learn what the pope's real belief concerning hell is, but there is no indication that Lawler thinks Francis is heterodox on the point. Armstrong continues with another such refutation, and then he draws a conclusion:

> This is the sort of "D+ in debating class" argumentation we find again and again in the book. Phil Lawler and legions of papal critics are perfectly sincere and well-meaning (I freely grant), but that doesn't free them from the responsibility of (at the very least) providing solid evidence in their critiques.

The problem is that Armstrong more than once misconstrues Lawler's critiques, thus making the grade of D+ undeserved and capricious. He continues his characterization of *Lost Shepherd*:

> Most of the book was actually taken up with gossipy, *National Enquirer*-like "palace intrigue" and internal affairs of cardinals and the curia and what Karl Keating in his glowing Facebook review called "administrative

or leadership style and actions" of the pope. . . . I've never had the slightest interest in such things (I don't watch soap operas). I was specifically looking to see how Phil would back up the extraordinary claims made in the introduction. In my opinion, he has absolutely failed to demonstrate that Pope Francis is deliberately trying to subvert or overthrow Catholic tradition. That hasn't been even remotely proven in this book.

Armstrong admits he takes no interest in internal Vatican machinations and doesn't care about what I styled the pope's "administrative or leadership style and actions" (which I didn't write in my "glowing Facebook review" but in a later Facebook post called "What Makes for a 'Bad Pope'?"), yet those are precisely the things that are the chief subjects in Lawler's book, in *The Dictator Pope*, and in *To Change the Church*. All three books devote far more pages to non-doctrinal matters than to doctrinal matters. In the middle of his book Lawler discusses the two-part synod that resulted in *Amoris Laetitia*. The relevant chapter is titled "Manipulating the Synod," and his point is that the pope, in consort with a few key advisors, choreographed the synod so that its proceedings, interim reports, and final result would reflect a preconceived plan rather than the full, open, and public deliberation of the synod fathers.

So it is throughout *Lost Shepherd*. Lawler argues that Francis has used a heavy hand in dealing with subordinates and, while praising collegiality among bishops, in fact has undercut episcopal cooperation. Lawler's assertions are either true, false, or a mixture, but such are his assertions, and they form the bulk of his book's argument. Armstrong takes no notice of them in his review, and he takes almost no notice of them in the remainder of his voluminous defense of Francis. His interest is in establishing the pope's doctrinal bona fides, while the chief interest of many of the critics he writes against lies elsewhere.

\* \* \*

On December 28, 2017, I wrote a Facebook post in which I was critical of Dave Armstrong's comments on *Lost Shepherd*. At that point he had not yet seen the book—Phil Lawler later sent him a pre-publication copy—but he had felt free to castigate it. What little he knew about it was from my earlier review[39] of it on Facebook.

I titled my post "One Friend of Mine Going After Another Regarding Pope Francis." Here is what I said:

> My recent post about Phil Lawler's upcoming book, *Lost Shepherd*, has generated over 300 comments and replies—and that's just on my Facebook timeline. My post has been shared elsewhere, and even more comments and replies have been written. I admit to being surprised. I also admit to disappointment regarding not a few of the comments. Most of the ones that disappoint me are from people I don't know, but several have been from my friend Dave Armstrong, the well-known apologist.

Today, at his Patheos page, Dave uploaded a very long piece called "Quasi-Defectibility and Phil Lawler vs. Pope Francis.[40] He added a link to his piece in the comment thread that follows my original post. ("Quasi-defectibility" is a term Dave made up.)

I think Dave's piece misconstrues Phil's book (which Dave admits he hasn't read), mischaracterizes Phil (as a reactionary out to "trash" the pope), and does a real disservice to the whole discussion. This is what I wrote as a comment at Patheos:

"Dave: You have done Phil Lawler a grave disservice in what you have written. You admit that your only knowledge of his upcoming book, *Lost Shepherd*, comes from my review of it. (I was sent and carefully read a pre-publication copy.) You haven't read the book yourself, yet you feel free to characterize it (really, mischaracterize it)—and Lawler. I expected more from you.

"You complain that people won't buy a book you wrote defending Pope Francis but they likely will buy 'a book that trashes the pope,' by which you mean Lawler's. First of all, his book doesn't 'trash' the pope at all (but you wouldn't know that since you haven't read it yet). It's a respectful examination, in considerable depth, of issues that people of various persuasions have called confusing or problematic or unbecoming.

"Second of all, your book[41] came out almost exactly four years ago, long before *Amoris Laetitia*, long before the synods, long before the personnel upheavals at the Vatican, long before the pope's management style became evident. I have looked at your book's table of contents: very few of the topics there are covered in Lawler's book, and almost nothing that he writes about is covered in yours.

"You seem piqued that his book is likely to sell far better than yours, and you seem to attribute the variance to defects in human nature, the implication being that people like to read downbeat rather than upbeat books. (You don't seem to take into account that your book's failure to see substantial sales may have quite different causes.)

"You accuse Lawler of 'doublethink' and virtually label him a reactionary (you say he uses reactionary methods), and you accuse him of holding something you call the 'quasi-defectibility' position. Such labeling doesn't clarify; it obscures—much as you would say that certain Traditionalists' use of 'neo-Catholic' to describe your position (or mine) obscures and doesn't clarify.

"But the use of an unhelpful term such as 'quasi-defectibility' is a lesser problem. A greater one is that you throw Lawler into the reactionary camp, which, on your scale, is the unsavory wing of Traditionalism. But Lawler isn't a reactionary at all (even though, granted, he is 'reacting' to certain papal actions), and I can't think of any Traditionalist Catholics who would label him even a Traditionalist. His book makes evident (something I already knew) that he is a man of conservative temperament, slow to draw conclusions, anxious to give Churchmen the benefit of the doubt. He is more a Russell Kirk than a Michael Voris.

"I'm quite disappointed at the way you have been handling this. You have let it appear that there is a personal element involved (as with your book), but mostly you have gone off half-cocked, have done a good man a bad turn, and have gotten not a few things just plain wrong. You seem too wrapped up in the controversy personally. I suggest you move on to something else. Please take down the tendentious commentary, give private thought to what you have written, and send Phil an apology."

Armstrong replied this way:

I didn't classify Phil as a reactionary, though I can see why someone would think so. I merely noted that in what I have been able to see so far in his book, he is thinking like one in some key/characteristic respects. In my Facebook discussions today, I clarified this very thing.

I don't know if Lawler is a reactionary or not. He may have crossed the line, or is close to it, and/or is about to do so. He has now (seemingly) come to a position that the reactionary sites have been maintaining for four years. I know, from the evidence presented thus far, that he is definitely thinking like them in this instance. That's not just me rambling off the top of my head. I've studied reactionaries for 25 years; written two books and scores and scores of articles about them. . . .

I haven't characterized the whole book because I haven't read it. I stated, "What exactly is Lawler claiming? What teaching of the Church is Pope Francis supposedly going to change? Well, we don't know for sure yet. The book comes out next February 26th." But the portions you cite are, to me, very serious and unwarranted charges. He believes that Pope Francis is "leading the Church away from the ancient sources of the Faith" and is "engaged in a deliberate effort to change what the Church teaches." Those are extremely serious accusations.

You're correct that my book on Pope Francis came out before most of the controversies about him took place. I can't change that fact. And there could be lots of reasons why it didn't sell apart from its optimistic nature (foremost among them, that it is self-published and has very little advertising). I was merely making a footnote point about what people like to buy: how they prefer "pessimistic" works to more optimistic and positive ones. It's easy as pie to provide evidence that strongly supports that contention. . . .

Quasi-defectibility is indeed a helpful opinion to analyze, because it is highly characteristic of reactionary thought. You don't critique my actual reasoning; you simply object to the term. But that's not an argument. If I simply tossed out the term as an epithet with no accompanying reasoning, you would have a legitimate point. But I don't do that. I explain exactly why I think so, by citing my book from 15 years ago.

I often argue in terms of analogy, and this is an extended example of that. Phil Lawler is increasingly arguing the way that reactionaries have in the past. That's simply a fact. And it is verified by the fact that the major reactionary sites (OnePeterFive, *The Remnant*, Rorate Caeli, LifeSite News) are increasingly extolling his work, as he has become more and more critical of the pope.

This is not insignificant. As an observer of these groups for over 25 years (and also with a sociological background—my college degree—that I often utilize in my apologetics work), I see the patterns of their behavior. Lawler appears to presently be their "darling" among us "neo-Catholics": the one they hope will come over to their side completely. If we want to see if a person is possibly heading down the road to reactionary Catholicism, we can look to see what the known reactionary sites are saying about him: if he is praised as having exceptional integrity, a cut above the other compromised "neo-Catholics," etc. And so we see that this is the case with Lawler. . . .

Lawler is [what I would call] bashing a pope. They like that and they see it. He's starting to question Vatican II. They (who despise Vatican II) like that and they see it. He's talking in quasi-defectibility terms. They resonate with that, too, and see it.

The trends are real and they are towards the right of the ecclesiological spectrum: towards Traditionalism and possibly in the future past that category, to radical reactionary Catholicism. He's not all the way there, but the ones who are see the signs and hope he will keep going all the way. Perfectly consistent.

Here I wish to note two things. Armstrong repeatedly asserts that critics of Pope Francis are on a trajectory and likely will end up arm-in-arm with Traditionalist Catholics who have been at loggerheads with the Vatican for decades. In this he largely agrees with our mutual friend Pete Vere, a former canon lawyer and apologist, who often has predicted that papal critics will move right through Traditionalism into sedevacantism.

Armstrong and Vere repeatedly write in terms of slipper slopes, though they have not identified individuals who, once having held responsible positions in what might be termed mainstream conservative Catholicism, have criticized Francis and then have found themselves moving across the spectrum and effectively out of the Church. (Louie Verrecchio, who is mentioned elsewhere in these pages, became a de facto sedevacantist long before *Amoris Laetitia* was issued and so is not an example of this supposed tendency.)

The second note I wish to make regards Armstrong's nomenclature. He likes to use labels such as "pope basher," but his favorite seems to be one of his own fashioning, "radical Catholic reactionary," which he sometimes abbreviates as "RadCathR." People so labeled he means to distinguish from Catholics who might call themselves Traditionalists only because they prefer the older rites, particularly of the Mass; such people might have no particular dislike or even interest in Pope Francis. By "radical Catholic reactionaries" Armstrong means instead people who write for, and who agree with what is written at, *The Remnant* and such websites as Steve Skojec's OnePeterFive,[42] Louie Verrecchio's akaCatholic,[43] and Rorate Caeli.[44]

I repeatedly have urged Armstrong to eschew labels such as "radical Catholic reactionary," arguing that they do little to clarify and that, like widely throw nets, they drag in the guilty as well as the innocent.

Back to his comments about Phil Lawler.

You apparently assume [Lawler] will stop at the point he is now, even though his past few years shows him becoming more and more "anti-Francis" and now he's considering taking a dim view of Vatican II as well. If he turns decisively against Vatican II, that will be two out of the four always-present hallmarks of the reactionaries (blasting the Ordinary Form and ecumenism being the other two).

He could also go the route of asserting that Francis is guilty of personal heresy or has (or soon will) bind the Church to it. If he does that, he would simply be following the path that the reactionary extremists have been on regarding all the popes since Pius XII: but more so, the later the pope.

Armstrong seldom writes about people who simply might be critical of the Ordinary Form of the Mass—that is, the vernacular version instituted in the wake of Vatican II. To him, people who prefer the old rite don't have mere reservations about the new rite. They "blast" it. Some people indeed "blast" it, at least in certain Traditionalist quarters. But not everyone—perhaps not most people—who find fault with the Ordinary Form ought to be accused of "blasting" it. After all, one such person was then-Cardinal Joseph Ratzinger.

Chris Ferrara at the notoriously reactionary site *The Remnant* praised Lawler in September 2016 (you'll never see them praise me!). The same thing is true of the reactionary site LifeSite News (they are praising Lawler) and Rorate Caeli. I'm sure we could find much more. I know how these people think. They latch onto any prominent persons in what they call the category of "neo-Catholicism" and see if they are becoming more Traditionalist and then onto their own reactionary Catholicism.

I've seen it time and again. So now one of their darlings is Phil Lawler. They hope and pray that he will fully join them. In the meantime, they'll keep praising him. Mark my words!

As one who is personally familiar with the trajectory of people like Robert Sungenis and Gerry Matatics (former employee of Catholic Answers [the apostolate I founded—KK]), it's remarkable to me that you don't see any of these warning signs. Time will tell, won't it?

Lawler's not a reactionary now, but he may yet be. And if he ends up there, I called it and warned people that it was coming, just as I warned people like Mario Derksen in 2000 that he was on the road to possible schism (he shortly thereafter became a sedevacantist, like Matatics). The reactionaries themselves think

[Lawler] is on the road, and so do I. I could be wrong, of course. I hope I am. But his book will do great damage whether he descends to full-fledged reactionary status or not. . . .

I tremble for Phil Lawler. James 3:1 states: "Let not many of you become teachers, my brethren, for you know that we who teach shall be judged with greater strictness." I have to stand accountable to God as an apologist for what I teach. God forbid that I lead anyone away from the pope and Church and spread any falsehood.

If I'm wrong in this, I am [wrong] out of a sincere desire to defend pope and Church. If I'm wrong about Pope Francis, then at least I have done all I can to give him every last benefit of the doubt. I will go down defending a pope rather than trashing him. I'll take that "wager" any day of the week.

The statements in the book of Pope Francis "leading the Church away from the ancient sources of the Faith" and his supposedly being "engaged in a deliberate effort to change what the Church teaches" are certainly garbage. You can classify that as whatever category you want, but it's undeniably garbage: especially without proof.

Here again Armstrong uses a label to close off an argument: "garbage." It is a word he uses repeatedly online to dismiss a book or article he disagrees with. The word has no substance in itself. It tells the reader nothing about the thing castigated. It is what rhetorician Richard Weaver called a "devil word": all it does is signify disapproval.

Keep in mind that at this point Armstrong had not yet seen *Lost Shepherd*. He was replying to my favorable comments about it. He had only my writing to go on, yet he felt able to say the book was "undeniably garbage." He continued:

> If you keep harping on the fact that I haven't read the whole book, then send me the damned thing (since you have it). I guarantee I will find more in it that is objectionable. As it is, the few statements you have shown us are outrageous and outlandish.

I replied to Armstrong this way:

> You say—on the basis of two short quotations—that Lawler's book is "undeniably garbage: especially without proof." How do you know what "proof" Lawler serves up? You haven't seen the book yet. You know none of its words beyond the few that I quoted. You don't know whether Lawler offers not one shred of proof (your assumption, clearly) or pages upon pages of proof.
>
> What you should have said is this: nothing. At this point, you have almost no information to go on

regarding the book, which is 256 pages long. I quoted well less than a page worth. If the tables were turned, you'd be outraged—and justifiably so.

It would be easy for someone looking at just a couple of sentences or phrases from one of your books to put an entirely unfair spin on it. Such a person could say, "Armstrong doesn't have a clue what he's talking about in this book," even though you might make a solid (not necessarily convincing or compelling) case for whatever your theme is. Such a person might well read into those few snippets from you things that simply aren't there—as you have with Lawler.

Armstrong objected: "I did not say the book was 'garbage' based on a few quotes. I said that those quotes were garbage. . . . You can classify [those quotations] as whatever category you want, but it's undeniably garbage: especially without proof."

I answered this way:

Fine, you meant only those two quotations, but even regarding them my point remains: you don't know what comes before and after them; you don't know if Lawler proffered reasons for those comments or just drew them out of a hat. Until you read the book, I think you should allow for the possibility that a fellow as otherwise astute as Lawler might have reasons that just haven't occurred to you yet. Then again, he might not. Since you can't know until you read the book, I don't think you should have made such heated comments.

Then this from Armstrong:

You can either send me the book, or you can keep harping on this theme of my essential unfairness because I haven't read it. Your choice.

* * *

At this juncture let me mention a name brought up by Armstrong, that of Christopher Ferrara. Armstrong complains that Ferrara, who is probably the most prolific writer at *The Remnant*, "praised Lawler" ("you'll never see them praise me!"). The parenthetical gripe no doubt is accurate, since Armstrong is not a Traditionalist, and *The Remnant* almost never says anything praiseworthy about non-Traditionalists.

Armstrong calls *The Remnant* "notoriously reactionary." However fair or unfair that characterization may be, I think it is fair to say that Ferrara often hyperventilates in his writing, especially when he is writing against someone or something, as in the following pair of paragraphs from an article titled "Pope Francis: A Pelagian Lutheran."[45]

As was noted at the outset of this piece, we cannot refrain from documenting the course of this disastrous papacy, unlike any in the entire history of the Church, including the pontificates of Paul VI and John Paul II. Nor can we ignore the obvious conclusion after five years of this insanity: that the Chair of Peter is currently occupied by a promoter of manifold heresy who has no respect for any teaching of the Church that contradicts his idiosyncratic mélange of populist piety and half-baked Modernism.

God alone, or perhaps a future pope or council, may someday judge whether Bergoglio fell from office on account of heresy or whether his election was valid in the first place. Meanwhile, we are left to cope with the ruinous effects of this pontificate while praying for its merciful termination, failing the conversion of a pope who has become the eye of a neo-Modernist hurricane now bearing down on the household of the Faith.

"Unlike any in the entire history of the Church"? I don't think Ferrara meant that in the pedestrian sense that every papacy is unlike every other one; each has distinctive notes. He meant it, apparently, in the sense that the Francis papacy is worse than any of the preceding 265 papacies. Such a claim would be hard to prove and would require not taking into consideration a fair number of popes from the Renaissance and the tenth century, at least.

When making his comparison, Ferrara, doesn't say,

"unlike any in the history of the Church, including John XII and Alexander VI," two popes that I mentioned earlier. Instead, he brackets Francis with Paul VI and John Paul II, as though those two were among the worst popes in history. No doubt some readers of *The Remnant* think they were, partly because those readers have been submerged in articles written against those two popes throughout the fifty years of the publication's existence and partly because those readers, like the unwashed masses of Catholics they distance themselves from, just don't know Church history. If your historical horizon goes back only to Vatican II, you don't have many popes to choose from in choosing the bad ones.

As for the Francis papacy as a whole, Ferrara calls it an "insanity" because, in his eyes, Francis promotes not an ambiguous formulation here and there but "manifold heresy"—that is to say, the pope promotes multiple heresies. Compare this to Phil Lawler, whom Dave Armstrong so severely castigates. Lawler states that Francis is not a heretic because he has promoted no heresy, even if he has authorized ambiguities. There isn't a small gap between Lawler's position and Ferrara's. There's a Grand Canyon.

Ferrara says that "God alone, or perhaps a future pope or council, may someday judge whether Bergoglio fell from office on account of heresy or whether his election was valid in the first place." There seem to be but two alternatives allowed here: either "Bergoglio" (notice Ferrara's use of the surname) has manifested himself as a heretic and thus has ceased to be pope (this mimics the thinking of sedevacantists) or he never was elected validly in the first place. The second possibility leads either to the notion that Benedict XVI still is pope, on the theory that he intended to resign but failed to pull off a valid resignation, or, assuming the resignation "took," that there has been no valid pope since the (failed) 2013 conclave—and here we're at sedevacantism again.

Armstrong has speculated that papal critics such as Phil Lawler and Ross Douthat will end up as sedevacantists, but that speculation is without warrant. He has built such a narrow redoubt that anyone outside it is far outside it. He is closer to reality in suggesting that some people associated with *The Remnant* likely will end up in sedevacantism, with Christopher Ferrara's name heading the list. Given Ferrara's hyperbolic language, which gets ever more hyperbolic the longer Francis reigns, Armstrong may be right. At least it looks as though Ferrara has worked himself into a tizzy regarding Francis, about whom he seems entirely incapable of writing objectively, and people in tizzies can end up in places even they don't think they're going.

That also means Ferrara has made his writing incapable of influencing anyone not already on *The Remnant* wavelength. This contrasts sharply with the books by Lawler and Douthat and even the one by Sire. Even Sire's book is tame compared to Ferrara's writing about the pope. The three books already have sold widely and likely will continue to sell well for some months. They will end up giving the overall tone to criticism of Pope Francis. They will be the books most people will read. *The Remnant* will have to be satisfied with just that, the remnant.

\* \* \*

Returning now to Dave Armstrong, I continued our discussion in a Facebook thread where I responded to a comment made by Pete Vere. I replied, "As I noted elsewhere, neither you nor Dave has much right, at this point, to criticize Lawler's book because neither of you has seen it. The two of you are making what truly is a knee-jerk response. Every book is open to criticism (save, perhaps, my own, of course!), but legitimate criticism comes only after a book has been read."

Armstrong popped in and said: "Well, Karl, now I will see it, so you can stop this silly rhetorical schtick. Phil has agreed to send me a copy." I answered:

> Dave, there's nothing silly or shticky about rebuking you (and others on this thread) for roundly condemning a book you haven't even seen. I haven't rebuked you or anyone else for siding with Pope Francis but for playing unfairly. When I was a magazine publisher, I never would have considered running a book review by someone who hadn't even read the book, and I couldn't imagine any other publisher doing so.
>
> I look forward to your review of Phil's book, but now you unavoidably will approach it with a high level of

prejudice. You've positioned yourself so that it will be difficult for a reader to think you're giving the book a fair shake. That's what happens with pre-judging. You've put yourself in a corner.

Many readers of your review will suspect that you have not referred to parts of Phil's argument that you found unexpectedly convincing and contrary to your initial prejudices and that you have given false emphasis to parts that confirm your pre-reading remarks, out of pride or stubbornness. Go ahead and write the review, but please know that many people—myself among them—will have to look at it in light of your peremptory condemnation.

A bit later I added this:

Phil Lawler, in his book, says that on some matters he has changed his mind about Pope Francis. That shouldn't lead anyone to suggest (as Pete has suggested) that it's evidence that Phil is moving in a theologically "reactionary" direction and that next he will be endorsing sedevacantism or some other goofiness.

As far as whether you condemned his whole book or only extracts, I think it's fair to say that the whole tenor of your initial remarks indicated that you disapproved of the whole book. That's how most readers would take what you said, even if that wasn't what you really meant. It's how I took it.

Even then, as I mentioned, the few sentences I quoted shouldn't have been condemned without first understanding their context, the context in these cases being several preceding pages (or more). It would have been fine if you had said something like "At first glance, I think I have to disagree with what Lawler is saying here, though I'll reserve final judgment until I've read the book. Maybe I'll end up rejecting nearly all of his argument. Maybe I'll end up accepting nearly all of it except for these extracts. We'll have to wait and see."

Armstrong replied:

Then when I get the book I will start critiquing parts of it (not all of it: I don't have the time or desire to do that). I have less than no interest in reading about or critiquing the pope's "bedside manner" and comportment. I'm interested in proof of what he is supposedly changing or seeking to change, that should not be changed.

Subsequent to this Armstrong produced a five-part critique of *Lost Shepherd*, but it was a critique of only a few portions of the book. The bulk of Lawler's text deals with what Armstrong dismissed as "the pope's 'bedside manner'"—that is, the way Francis has undertaken—or failed to undertake—reform of the curia, how he has dealt with ecclesiastics with whom he has had disagreements, such as Cardinals Burke and Müller, how he has scolded, repeatedly, prelates who gathered to hear his addresses, and how he otherwise has conducted himself in public and in private.

Armstrong said he had "less than no interest in reading about or critiquing" such things, which is fine, but his wholesale condemnation of Lawler's book (and similarly of the criticisms or books of others) is based on too little of the text. His most extended look at *Lost Shepherd* was distributed over five articles at his blog: "Lawler vs. Pope Francis #1: Critique of Introduction";[46] "Lawler vs. Pope Francis #2: Homosexuality & 'Judging'";[47] "Lawler vs. Pope Francis #3: The Pope Annihilated Hell?";[48] "Lawler vs. Pope Francis #4: Communion/Buenos Aires Letter";[49] and "Lawler vs. Pope Francis #5: Jerusalem Council vs. 'Ideology.'"[50]

The fifth article, which is representative of the other four, considers less than one page in Lawler's book; there he questions Pope Francis's interpretation of an episode in the Book of Acts. Lawler thinks the pope lets it appear that he considers that those Christians "who disagreed with St. Paul on the enforcement of Mosaic Law" (St. James among them) "were not believers." This comes in a section of the book in which Lawler writes about what he considers to be the pope's hyperbolic language.

It is not a particularly important point, one to which

Lawler devotes 258 words over two paragraphs before moving on. Armstrong's critique comes to 2,649 words, more than ten times the text being criticized. Similarly with the other four articles, which, cumulatively, examine only a few pages of *Lost Shepherd*. Armstrong attacks them with a rigor entirely out of proportion to their page count or to their relative importance in the book.

Taken together, the five articles are Armstrong's most sustained critique of *Lost Shepherd*, yet they take into account not even a tenth of it. He blithely dismisses (has "less than no interest in") the more important parts of the author's argument. Armstrong may rightly boast that "I've been the most vocal critic of Phil Lawler's pathetic book *Lost Shepherd*," but one legitimately might wonder whether *pathetic* applies more properly to the book or to its critique.

\* \* \*

Dave Armstrong repeatedly has claimed that he has written more in defense of Pope Francis—and more against the pope's critics—than anyone in the blogosphere, and he probably is right. He says he has written well over one hundred posts (some of them thousands of words long) defending not just Francis but himself as a defender of Francis. Here is his own overview of his approach to dealing with popes and criticisms of them. It appeared as his Patheos blog site under the title "On Rebuking Popes & Catholic Obedience to Popes."[51] I intersperse my own observations.

My position is that popes should be accorded the proper respect of their office and criticized rarely, by the right people, in the right spirit, preferably in private Catholic venues, and for the right (and super-important) reasons. Virtually none of those characteristics hold for most of the people moaning about the pope day and night these days.

I've lived to see an age where an orthodox Catholic apologist defending the pope (for the right reasons) is regarded as some sort of novelty or alien from another galaxy. Truth is stranger than fiction!

Being classified as an ultramontanist is almost a boilerplate response from critics of a given pope. It's very common to reply to defenses of a pope or papal authority by making out that one supposedly agrees with absolutely everything he says or does, or that his color of socks or what side of bed he gets out on or his favorite ice cream flavor are magisterial matters.

It's true that Armstrong, Pete Vere, and others have been called ultramontanists by some critics of Pope Francis, but I don't recall seeing anyone use the term in the silly sense in which Armstrong defines it here. He would have trouble pointing to anyone who thinks he thinks the pope is infallible in choosing between vanilla and chocolate ice cream. In other words, he exaggerates. Those who label him an ultramontanist (improperly, I think) are saying by the use of that term that they think he is insufficiently critical, in the good sense of that term, that he gives Francis more leeway than is warranted, given well-established facts concerning certain incidents, and that Armstrong plumps for a far-fetched understanding of something the pope has said or done rather than the obvious, everyday understanding.

Certainly there are authentic ultramontanists. Their patron saint might be William George Ward (1812-1882), a convert and the grandfather of Maisie Ward, wife of Frank Sheed and, with him, founder of the publishing house Sheed & Ward. The elder Ward perhaps is most famous for having remarked, "I would like to have a papal bull every morning with my *Times* at breakfast." He brooked no opposition to the occupant of the See of Peter and is not remembered as ever having been a critic of any pope. (It remains unknown whether he looked forward to a bull regarding ice cream.)

Back to Armstrong:

It's untrue in my case, as I will show; this has never been my position, as I've explained many times. But if it is erroneously thought that it is, then I can be potentially (or actually) dismissed as a muddled, simplistic irrelevancy, without my arguments being fully engaged. Nice try, but no cigar.

It was Cardinal Newman who fought most valiantly against the ultramontanist mindset: opposing those such as Cardinal Manning and William G. Ward (also sometimes known as neo-ultramontanists). Cuthbert Butler, the historian of Vatican I, described Ward's view as follows:

"He held that the infallible element of bulls, encyclicals, etc., should not be restricted to their formal definitions but ran through the entire doctrinal instructions; the decrees of the Roman Congregation, if adopted by the Pope and published with his authority, thereby were stamped with the mark of infallibility, in short 'his every doctrinal pronouncement is infallibly rendered by the Holy Ghost.'"

This has never remotely been my view. Before I converted, as a card-carrying Evangelical, I opposed the notion of infallibility itself tooth and nail, despised the view as hopelessly naïve and false to history. It was my biggest objection: infinitely more so than Mary or things like Tradition or infused justification. I read Döllinger, Küng, and George Salmon in order to try to disprove it.

Thus, I was not at all predisposed, as a young convert, to ultramontanism. That would be the very last thing likely to happen. In fact, if that were what Catholicism required, I highly doubt that I would have become a Catholic at all. Cardinal Newman wrote (and I totally agree):

"To submit to the Church means this, first you will receive as *de fide* whatever she proposes *de fide.* . . . You are not called on to believe *de fide* any thing but what has been promulgated as such. You are not called on to exercise an internal belief of any doctrine which sacred congregations, local synods, or particular bishops, or the pope as a private doctor, may enunciate. You are not called upon ever to believe or act against the moral law, at the command of any superior."[52]

Thus far, all Catholics who aren't dissidents or Modernists agree, even in our crazy day and age. The hard part comes when Newman discusses obedience and deference to the pope:

"I say with Cardinal Bellarmine whether the pope be infallible or not in any pronouncement, anyhow he is to be obeyed. No good can come from disobedience. His facts and his warnings may be all wrong; his deliberations may have been biased. He may have been misled. Imperiousness and craft, tyranny and cruelty, may be patent in the conduct of his advisers and instruments.

"But when he speaks formally and authoritatively he speaks as our Lord would have him speak, and all those imperfections and sins of individuals are overruled for that result which our Lord intends (just as the action of the wicked and of enemies to the Church are overruled) and therefore the pope's word stands, and a blessing goes with obedience to it, and no blessing with disobedience."[53]

His thought was echoed by Venerable Pope Pius XII, in his encyclical *Humani Generis* (1950):

"Nor must it be thought that what is expounded in encyclical letters does not of itself demand consent, since in writing such letters the popes do not exercise the supreme power of their teaching authority. For these matters are taught with the ordinary teaching authority, of which it is true to say: 'He who hears you, hears me,' and generally what is expounded and inculcated in encyclical letters already for other reasons appertains to Catholic doctrine. But if the supreme pontiffs in their official documents purposely pass judgment on a matter up to that time under dispute, it is obvious that that matter, according to the mind and will of the same pontiffs, cannot be any longer considered a question open to discussion among theologians."[54]

*Lumen Gentium* (Dogmatic Constitution on the Church), from Vatican II (1964) also reiterates the same notion:

"This religious submission of mind and will must be shown in a special way to the authentic magisterium of the Roman pontiff, even when he is not speaking *ex cathedra*; that is, it must be shown in such a way that his supreme magisterium is acknowledged with reverence, the judgments made by him are sincerely adhered to, according to his manifest mind and will. His mind and will in the matter may be known either from the character of the documents, from his frequent repetition of the same doctrine, or from his manner of speaking."[55]

Apparently some detractors of Pope Francis think I accept every jot and tittle of everything he says and that all popes say. This is untrue. Five minutes spent at the search box on my blog (which contains over 2,000 papers, so that none of my views are exactly secrets) would have easily disproved this notion. But we're all busy. . . .

I'm sure there were also many instances of morally inferior popes (e.g., during the Renaissance) being soundly rebuked by holy priests and laymen. This is nothing novel whatsoever in Catholic ecclesiology. No one knows better than Catholics the distinction between the nobility of an office and (too often) the sanctity of the person holding it at any given time. . . .

My main objection today is the spirit in which many objections to Pope Francis are made. That has often been my critique through the years of papal criticism, which I have always maintained is quite permissible in and of itself, done in the right way, at the right time, with proper respect, by the right people, in the right venue, privately, and with the right motivation. My position is not one in which popes can never be criticized, but rather, a concern about how, when, and who does it: the proper way to do it.

If I am asked today whether these conditions as I understand them have been met, I reply with a definite "No!" We have all over the place (most of them otherwise orthodox and obediently Catholic) a spirit of individual complaining and moaning about the pope and accusations quite often not substantiated or proven.

I see a lack of deference and obedience that reminds me (as radical reactionary Catholics always have) of either theologically liberal, dissident Catholicism (which disdains the pope and many things he says) and/or Protestantism (which disdains the pope and many things he says but at least never made any pretense of following him). The people doing it invariably don't intend to think and act like folks in one of those categories, but seem unaware that they have partially adopted their spirit. . . .

These last three paragraphs put great restrictions on who may criticize a pope and when. Armstrong says that any criticism ought to be "done in the right way" (which he otherwise does not define), "at the right time" (also left indeterminate), "by the right people" (he seems to think that this constitutes a very small group, perhaps those in orders and certain scholars), and "privately."

Certainly there is great promiscuity today in complaints about the pope—and not just the current pope but his several predecessors, going back at least to Paul VI. There was a time when the everyday Catholic might tut-tut about a pope, but he would not think to making his thoughts public, sharing them only with confidants. In those days, most laymen never learned enough about what popes did or said because news about papal thoughts and actions was sparse. There were no Vatican press conferences. If popes left Rome, it was for their summer stay at Castel Gandolfo. (Paul VI was the first pope to travel by airplane. He flew to Jordan and Israel in 1964.) There were no papal extravanganzas in foreign countries and certainly nothing like World Youth Day. The pope's visage seldom was in the newspapers and even less frequently in the newsreels.

Although the popes were the head of the world's most populous religious body, they lived rather private lives. If a pope happened to say something untoward or failed in dealing properly with his subordinates, the fault usually didn't pass beyond the walls of the Vatican. If such a pope required correction, the correction could be done privately. At most a few higher clerics ever would learn of the matter.

Today's situation is quite different, partly because of changes in external circumstances but largely because of papal choice. Francis, with more alacrity than John Paul II or Benedict XVI, consents to interviews, sometimes at his residence in Casa Santa Marta, sometimes aboard airliners. He doesn't just consent to them: he initiates them. When he says something such as "Who am I to judge?", his words don't remain behind the Bronze Doors of the Apostolic Palace. They go out to all the world. They are not uttered privately, so a private correction would seem to be inapt. They are heard or read by millions, not a few of whom have the stature and composure to formulate responses that are at once respectful and on point.

Dave Armstrong sets out requirements for papal reproval. Some of those requirements may be as applicable today as they were half a century ago. Others not, external situations having changed. He says, "If I am asked today whether these conditions as I understand them have been met, I reply with a definite 'No!'" Perhaps his "No" should take into account changed conditions—some of which, as I said, have been changed by the popes themselves. Armstrong's strictures are so strict that almost no one will qualify to criticize a pope. This goes contrary, I think, to the nearly universal sense that, recent popes deliberately having opened themselves up to the public, they also have opened themselves to remonstrances that in earlier days would have been proffered by only a select few.

Let me refer to a still earlier paragraph quoted by Armstrong, the one in which John Henry Newman says, "I say with Cardinal Bellarmine whether the pope be infallible or not in any pronouncement, anyhow he is to be obeyed."

Newman makes clear what he means. Even if a pope weighs facts poorly and makes a wrong determination about a course of action, his orders are to be obeyed (unless, of course, he were to order a sinful action: something Newman hardly needed to mention here). This is true as far as it goes; it was true in Newman's time, and it is true in our time, but some Catholics take it too far. They say that to criticize a pope is to be disobedient to him.

I have seen this repeatedly in comments at Facebook. Well-intentioned Catholics, jealous of papal prerogatives and knowledgeable about Church history, recoil at any criticism of Pope Francis and argue against it in terms of obedience, but obedience is not the same as agreement or intellectual submission.

If the pope, speaking offhandedly, says something that is taken by many to be contrary to earlier Church teachings (even though he didn't intend any such understanding), it is not an exercise in obedience to say nothing about it. Obedience is not relevant to the matter. One might be right or wrong in judging that something a pope has said or written is right or wrong, but judging one way or the other has nothing to do with obedience. In many of these cases, where one discussant (usually online) brings up obedience, the hope is for discussion to be squelched by an appeal to an instinct common to orthodox Catholics.

Back to Armstrong.

> Even if I agreed that Pope Francis was some terrible heretic or (the more subtle argument today) that he

is a conspiratorial-type, tricky, conniving subversive, I would say that this ought to be discussed in private by bishops and the most eminent, orthodox theologians (and those revered as holy persons), not in public every day by anyone and everyone, all making out that they are qualified experts who may and can do so.

The latter is scandalous and a disgrace. It makes Catholics a laughingstock to the observing non-Catholic world. But apparently, the people who persist in doing this never think of that. It appears to never occur to them that private discussions (if they must continue this) would be far more prudent and wise. . . .

Again, I appreciate Armstrong's intentions here—most people truly are unqualified to discuss most issues, whether on religion or some other topic, though that seldom seems to have stopped anyone—but he doesn't address whether complete silence itself might be "scandalous and a disgrace." There are times when people with sufficient knowledge and skill may be obliged, in charity, to make their concerns known, even publicly. Such people are not limited to clerics resident in Rome.

I don't think it means we can never ever say anything critical, but it's talking about a spirit and outlook of respect and deference that is now widely being ignored, because people have learned to think in very un-Catholic ways, having (in my opinion) been too influenced by secular culture and theologically liberal and Protestant ways of thinking about authority and submission.

The sublimity of the office demands that we show respect and (almost always) shut up, even if the pope is wrong. If there are serious questions, bishops and theologians and canon lawyers (as I've always said) ought to discuss it privately, not publicly. . . .

But mostly people seem to just reflect whatever the media says, which is a real tragedy because we know the rotgut that the mainstream media spews. With Pope Francis it has become what I describe as a "narrative" that he is always supposedly saying stupid, offensive, confusing, or liberal things. It just keeps getting bigger like the snowball rolling downhill. So many are jumping on the bandwagon.

But as I have said, I've looked closely at many of these so-called "incidents" or allegedly "controversial" things and found that there was nothing seriously wrong at all. Then of course I get accused of "defending the pope no matter what, because you feel that you have to [i.e., as a Catholic apologist]." Can't win for losing in this field. It's a lot like being an umpire: you're always gonna make someone unhappy. . . .

I have defended Pope Francis. I don't assert that he is perfect (no one is). I don't even deny that he has possibly done or taught some incorrect/wrong things. But what I do is defend him, generally speaking (and in many particulars, which have been exposed as bum raps), and refuse to speak evil of him or criticize (rashly or otherwise), per the above reasons. Who am I to do so?

If indeed I am wrong at length, or as history ultimately judges, I'd much rather be wrong sincerely defending the pope than wrong bashing and lying about him week in and week out (if that is the truth of the matter). I think God would look a lot more kindly at my mistake (if it is one in his eyes) than those who operate and think on other terms, if they turn out to be wrong in the final analysis.[56]

\* \* \*

Around the first of the year the term "bad pope" began popping up in online discussions regarding the new books about Pope Francis. The first to use the term seems to have been Leila Lawler, wife of the author of *Lost Shepherd*. She said Phil agreed with her use of the term.

On the Feast of the Epiphany I wrote the following post at Facebook. Its title was "What Makes for a 'Bad Pope'?"

Apologist Dave Armstrong is in the midst of a series of chapter-by-chapter critiques of Phil Lawler's forthcoming book, *Lost Shepherd*. I mentioned that book here a few days ago. Dave and Phil are friends of mine. Phil is critical of Pope Francis, and Dave has taken it upon himself to counter Phil's arguments. The book isn't scheduled to be released until next month, but Phil sent Dave a galley proof of the book, and that is what Dave has been working from.

Another mutual friend, Pete Vere, a Canadian who some years ago worked in canon law and, on the side, in apologetics, has come to Dave's support. Like Dave, Pete thinks popes ought not to be criticized, except in extraordinary situations (the current situation not being one of them). Over the last few days Pete has complained about a comment made by Phil's wife, Leila. In a Facebook comment she said that she and Phil had concluded that Francis is a "bad pope." She didn't elaborate.

Pete responded by saying that he suspects that she and Phil entered the discussion with that point of view and thus have shown an unwarranted bias, whereas Dave, who has voiced nary a reservation about the pope, is writing objectively and without preconceptions. It was at this point that I decided to respond to Pete this morning, and I did so in these words:

"Some of these things you should be asking Phil and Leila Lawler directly, not me, because they involve the development of their perspectives on the pope, and I'm not privy to that information. Given Phil's early appreciation of Francis and his slowness in altering that, I think that what you term their 'intentions' regarding the pope actually are their judgments about him.

"From what I can see, they didn't begin with disappointment in him, but disappointment developed over several years. Leila says they now think he has been a 'bad pope,' a term that can be taken several ways, none of which her comment specified. If you read Phil's book (I gather you still haven't done so), you'll see that most of it concerns the pope's administrative or leadership style and actions, as shown not just since becoming pope but when he was in Argentina.

"If a pope is personally orthodox, even at times writing and speaking winningly about the Faith, but also is heavy-handed, vindictive, ill-judging in episcopal promotions, unjust in dealing with subordinates (whether, say, Cardinal Burke or the priests at CDF whom the pope told Cardinal Müller to fire without explanation either to him or to them)—is such a man a "bad pope"? . . .

"So in what way do Phil and Leila think Francis has been a 'bad pope'? I think they mean this in terms not of his teaching—as I said, Phil clearly states that Francis isn't a heretic—but of his non-doctrinal actions (excepting here the disarray caused by portions of *Amoris Laetitia*). Is it legitimate for them, or for other Catholics, to conclude that Francis, so far, has been less than a success—or even less than adequate—on the non-teaching side, to the point where he could be denominated a 'bad pope'? I suppose that depends on how one weighs the evidence, what one thinks is important versus insignificant.

"Does it tell us anything that Cardinal Müller wasn't informed that his five-year appointment wasn't going to renewed until the very day it expired, an unprecedented snub? Was this a sign of papal pettiness, indicative of a wider attitudinal problem? The answer is either Yes or No. I can imagine that some who answer Yes regarding that incident and a dozen others could conclude that, on the whole and so far, this has been a failed papacy and that Francis is a "bad pope"—not a bad man, not a sinful man (beyond what any pope, being human, would be), but nevertheless a man not suited to the role."

\* \* \*

This comment[57] by Pete Vere packs more into itself than might first appear—and more than Pete might realize: "This is why I am more offended by so-called orthodox Catholics who refer to the Holy Father as 'Pope Frank,' 'Bergoglio,' or a 'bad pope'."

I'd say the three examples he lists are not at the same level.

1. I remember some people referring to Benedict XVI affectionately as "Pope Benny," but, from my experience, when a diminutive is used of a pope—such as "Pope Frank"—almost always it's used as a put-down of the man as a man and thus just isn't warranted. (Worse, it seems childish: name calling always does. "And so's your ol' man!") It always has struck me as obtuse for someone who wants to criticize—whether the object of his criticism is a pope, a politician, or some other public figure—to refer to the target by his first name (this presumes the two don't actually know one another), particularly when there is an element of snark attached. It's easy to distinguish the positive sense in which "Pope Benny" was meant from the negative sense in which "Pope Frank" is meant. Why do those who speak this way do so? Don't they realize that they draw no one to their side, no matter how cogent the words that follow "Pope Frank"? Their online followers may chortle in unison—and they do—but I doubt a single convert it made to the anti-"Pope Frank" cause, and it's likely that some one-time followers, who still may have a sense of fair play, become no-time followers. The result is that the person who writes "Pope Frank" and the like ends up with a smaller following, not a larger. The tactic is self-defeating, so why do some persist in it? I can ask the question but can give no sufficient answer, not being a psychologist.

2. A usage such as "Pope Bergoglio" may or may not

show disrespect. I remember I became aware of such a usage, many years ago, when I saw in print "Pope Montini" (Paul VI). My reaction was that the usage was impolite, yet it appeared in a respectable journal. I was puzzled but came to see that in Italy and certain other countries, chiefly romance-language countries, it long has been customary to refer to popes by their family names rather than by (or in addition to) their regnal names. This may have something to do with the historical emphasis put on family ties in those cultures. Thus "Pope Roncalli," "Pope Pacelli," and the like. You find it not just in quotidian journalism but in respectable books too.

This is a usage unknown in English-speaking countries, at least as a usage of respect. When an American or Englishman writes about "Pope Bergoglio," unless the writer is trying to polish his I-live-in-Rome credentials, he's probably meaning it as a dig toward the pope. In many cases, of course, it's quite clear that that is what he's doing (just look at Traditionalist websites), and in any case other English speakers likely will take it that way, since many of them aren't aware of the Continental usage. An innocent use may be construed as an abuse.

3. What about "bad pope"? Pete Vere said he's offended by the term, but I don't think one should be. It's qualitatively different from the other two terms on his list. They hardly rise above the ad hominem, at least for English speakers, but "bad pope" isn't so much a substitute for a title as an evaluation. Yes, some people will throw it around just to show disrespect—and just because they can. But

"bad pope" is no more problematic than "good pope," which is a term Vere himself has used for Pope Francis.

A man can be a "bad pope" and yet a saint. The best example is Celestine V (reigned 1294), a canonized saint but truly a failure as pope—at least an administrative failure. He was the last pope to resign prior to Benedict XVI. He was "bad" in his administration of the Church because, in his innocence (he was elderly and had been a monk in the mountains east of Rome), he just didn't know how to lead any organization, let alone the Church, and things fell into disarray under his pontificate.

Saying that Celestine was a "bad pope" doesn't mean he was a bad man. In his case, he was a very good man indeed: thus the canonization. It's like saying that Millard Fillmore was a "bad president." Most historians agree that he was, but they don't say that he was a bad man, morally or otherwise. They say that for reasons partly outside his control and partly within his control, he failed to make of the presidency what he should have. Much the same has been said about other American presidents—and not necessarily out of partisan bias. Some presidents who had been senators or governors should have remained senators or governors, for the sake of the country and for their own sakes.

Usually, when the term "bad pope" is voiced, most people think about popes who notoriously broke the Sixth and Ninth Commandments during their pontificates: about half a dozen popes so qualify. This is not to be construed as meaning that popes have not broken any of the other Commandments, but it's an indication of a mindset, one that probably stems from America's Protestant (and, early on, Puritan) culture.

Even nowadays, when the term "scandal" comes up, Protestants tend to think of sexual lapses, while Catholics tend to think of giving bad examples. Both are wrong. "Scandal" comes from a Greek word meaning to be tripped up, as when a stone trips you up while walking along a path. There you are, your thoughts on other things, when suddenly your foot catches the stone and you're thrown off the path or onto your face. The stone has prevented you from reaching your goal. A religious leader could give scandal to his flock without breaking any of the Commandments, if his actions were such as to throw his charges off the spiritual path they were on.

Unfortunately, the term "bad pope" has come to have a limited connotation, so at first glance most people, at least in English-speaking countries, will imagine that something salacious gives rise to the term, but that need not be the case at all. There have been good men who have been bad presidents, and there is no reason why there could not be good men who end up as bad popes. That's at the theoretical level, of course. It is one thing to throw out the term; it is another to establish whether using it has any warrant.

Whether Francis will prove to have been a "bad pope" is something we shall learn eventually. Some people think he already has earned that description. Others think he hasn't remotely done so and will be remembered not as a "bad pope" but as a "good pope." Even today some of his defenders refer to him, in uppercase, as Good Pope Francis, much as admirers of John XXIII used to refer to him as Good Pope John. Someday we'll know which epithet for Francis is closer to reality.

These are matters of evaluation. I realize that those who might call the present Holy Father "Pope Frank" or (in an American usage) might refer to him simply as "Bergoglio" probably already have decided that he is a "bad pope," but their doing so doesn't diminish the permissibility of using a designator such as "bad pope" if one has grounds to argue that, somewhat like Celestine, Francis has confused things administratively or, not so much like Celestine, has personality defects or interpersonal skills that work against the smooth running of the Church.

It is in these latter senses, I believe, that Leila Lawler and her husband, Phil, have used the term "bad pope." To my recollection, it's not a term that appears in Phil's book, *Lost Shepherd*. I believe Leila was the first of the Lawlers to use it, in a Facebook comment, and in a later comment she said it reflected her view and Phil's.

So, going back to the beginning, I'd say that Pete Vere's list has three quite distinct elements. The way he lists them makes it seem that the three are at the same level of inappropriateness, but I'd say that only one truly is inappropriate (except in the "Pope Benny" sense of an endearment), one is inappropriate in some cultures but not in others, and one normally isn't inappropriate at all, when used as a conclusion to a train of thought.

# Chapter 3

# The Papal Gambler

The third of the trio of books that form the backbone of this book is Ross Douthat's *To Change the Church*. Let me begin by noting a few factual errors in it.

Chapter 1 begins this way: "At the center of earthly Catholicism, there is one man: the Bishop of Rome, the Supreme Pontiff, the Vicar of Christ, the Patriarch of the West, the Servant of the Servants of God, the 266th (give or take an anti-pope) successor of Saint Peter."[58] Fine, except "Patriarch of the West" was dropped as a papal title in 2006.

Later Douthat says, when writing about John Paul II and Vatican II, that "the only four bishops who were actually excommunicated under his papacy were the council's reactionary critics."[59] The reference is to the 1988 episcopal consecrations of four priests of the Society of St. Pius X, but it wasn't just the four who, under canon law, automatically were excommunicated. So were the two bishops who consecrated them, Marcel Lefebvre and Antonio de Castro Mayer, making the total number of excommunications six rather than four.

Much later in the book Douthat refers to Augustine as "the Church's most ancient and greatest Father."[60] Whether he is the greatest of the men so denominated is a matter of opinion, but it hardly can be a matter of opinion that Augustine, who died in 430, is the "most ancient" of the Fathers of the Church. That label usually is granted to the fourth pope, Clement I, who was martyred just before the end of the first century. And there are more Fathers between Clement and Augustine.

I point out these errors at the outset because it is proper to note that *To Change the Church* is an imperfect book. (These errors ought to have been caught by copy-editors and proofreaders—and by Douthat himself.) Perhaps there are other small errors that I missed in my reading, but on the whole the book—which has 135 footnotes—does a good job in making its case. It is a case that not every reader will accept, at least not entirely, but it is a reasonable case, given the evidence proffered.

Writing at Law & Liberty, a website of the Liberty Fund, Paul Seaton, who teaches at St. Mary's Seminary and University in Baltimore, said this about *To Change the Church*:

Douthat writes with sustained lucidity and even gracefulness. I would say that "he writes like an angel," but he is very much flesh and blood, as a cryptic allusion to an ongoing illness indicates. But he's flesh and blood of a rare sort, exhibiting equanimity in controversy and a desire to understand, above all. He is also not given to imputing the worst motives to those he critiques. He very much takes the high road. . . .

In *To Change the Church*, Ross Douthat has freely exercised his Catholic conscience. Remarkably, perhaps paradoxically, certainly not without doubts and reservations, he has turned his critical intelligence towards the head of his communion. Exhibiting many of the virtues that the Catholic intellect should possess, including respect for facts as well as persons, he has come to a most troubling conclusion. This is a significant contribution to an on-going intramural Catholic civil war.[61]

I think Seaton has the measure of Douthat and his book. Of the three works examined at length in these pages—*The Dictator Pope*, *Lost Shepherd*, and *To Change the Church*—the latter is the most docilely written, having almost no tendentious adjectives, no obvious "side" to push, yet it reaches a conclusion—at least a tentative conclusion—that some admirers of Pope Francis will resist. Douthat makes this last point himself.

He says there are "reasons to doubt all of the Francis era's competing visions for the Church:"

the conservatives' because the Church has changed in the past more than they are often ready to admit, the Traditionalists' because the Church has needed to change more than they seem ready to allow, and the liberals' because it is hard to see how the Church can change in the ways that they envision without cutting itself off from its own history and abandoning its claim to carry a divine message, an unchanging truth.[62] . . .

Finally, there are Catholic readers who will find this book's critical portrait of a sitting pope to be inappropriate, impious, disloyal. They may be right; there I must rely on the mercy of God, which Francis has so eloquently stressed, if I have strayed into presumption and failed in the religious duties I assumed when I converted twenty years ago.[63]

The main text of Douthat's book is 210 pages long. It isn't until thirty percent in, with the chapter titled "The Francis Agenda," that a real consideration of the present papacy begins. Before that Douthat gives mainly historical background, looking at Vatican II, the abdication of Benedict XVI, and the 2013 conclave that resulted in a surprise choice.

In a section discussing reactions to early writings of Pope Francis, such as his encyclical *Evangelii Gaudium* ("The Joy of the Gospel"), Douthat says, "But among conservative and Traditionalist Catholics, where John Paul and Benedict had seen the seeds of a renewed and vigorous Church, the new pope saw a great many Pharisees and scribes."[64] This became more evident in the pope's oral remarks, whether in prepared addresses or in offhand comments.

"To be sure," said Douthat, "there were legalists in their [conservatives'] ranks; to be sure there were stone-throwers and nostalgists and bigots; to be sure the temptation toward self-righteousness was ever-present, ever-real."

But looking at the big picture, it seemed unfair to treat their beleaguered subculture—the homeschooling families raising five children on a modest budget, the young men joining the priesthood in a world that sneered at celibacy, the clusters of Catholics praying the rosary at abortion clinics, the elderly parishioners sacrificing to keep Eucharist adoration going—as if it shared all the authoritarian faults of the Church in Franco's Spain or Eamon de Valera's Ireland.

Especially since it was this subculture that in many cases had kept Catholicism in the West going, kept it from sharing Mainline Protestantism's fate, kept parishes from closing and seminaries from emptying, kept the Church's schools from going under and the Church's charities from becoming simple clients of the government, kept the Church's scandal-plagued bishops form becoming generals without an army.[65]

Douthat's sixth chapter is titled "The Marriage Problem." It deals with the dual synods on the family. He gives a fair overview of the Church's traditional teaching on marriage and divorce (yes to one, no to the other), grounding his survey in Scripture and history. He notes that the breakaway Orthodox churches have accepted divorce and remarriage, though with limitations on how many remarriages are permitted. Protestants, not seeing matrimony as sacramental, have no such limits. "Again and again, ecumenical councils—famous ones like Trent, forgotten ones like the Second Council of Lyon—declared that the Church cannot accept either the Orthodox compromise or the Protestant alternative."[66] But clearly some bishops at the synods wanted an alternative of some kind, and Douthat says that those bishops—headed by Cardinal Walter Kasper of Germany—not only had the pope's ear but his patronage. They disproportionately had leadership roles in the synods and through backroom maneuvering had disproportionate influence in the wording of its interim documents.

In the end, says Douthat, if may have been "a case of Francis trying to mediate between conservatives and liberals—letting the liberal wing of the Church make its case, and then doing some reform around annulments that would annoy rigorists but remain a theologically acceptable compromise." So conservatives told themselves, but "[t]hey were wrong, understandably but badly so. But it would take some time for this to become apparent."[67]

The following chapter of *To Change the Church* is titled, well, "To Change the Church." "How does one change an officially unchanging Church?" asks Douthat. "How does one alter what is not supposed to be in your power to remake? One answer: very carefully and by overwhelming consensus."[68]

> To be an instrument of change, the synodal process would need careful steering, the bishops involved would need to be selected carefully and then nudged, and the pope himself would have to make his desires clear without making them official. Which, during the months when conservative Catholics were reassuring themselves that he had no intention of touching anything doctrinal around marriage, is what Pope Francis and his inner circle set out to do.[69] . . .

> [W]hile the more liberal Catholics talked about the wonderful, spirit-filled working of the synodal process, the more conservative Catholics complained it had been rigged or otherwise manipulated. But many of them still stopped short of drawing the obvious conclusion—that any "rigging" had been conducted with the full approval of the man in charge and that everything from the design of the synod to the shocking *relatio* to the final decision on which paragraphs to include reflected the pope's own personal intentions, not the freelancing of the men who ran it, Archbishop [Bruno] Forte and Cardinal [Lorenzo] Baldisseri.[70]

There were many who, complaining about the course of the two synods, said that "the problem was not the pope himself; it could not be the pope himself. It was just the men around him, whose ambitions had pushed the synod process off the path that the Holy Father himself preferred."

This argument was not really credible, even if it was the only way that some conservative Catholics could reconcile their abiding papalism with the evidence of their eyes and ears. In the period around the synod, as in others during Francis's pontificate, you got a truer assessment from the Catholic fringes, the theological radicals on the left and the Latin Mass Traditionalists on the right, where skepticism of the papacy ran highest, than from the more mainstream Catholic experts.

You also got a truer assessment from the secular press: they might be biased in Francis's favor and unconcerned with the theological stakes, but their "reformist pope at war with reactionary Vatican" narrative still captured the reality of the Church's conflict better than either blithe "the Spirit is moving" liberals or anxious "but don't blame the pope" conservatives.[71]

Douthat notes a reversal of roles that likely has surprised most commentators across the theological spectrum. "After years of using 'the magisterium has spoken, the case is closed' as an argument ender, conservative Catholics now sided with the reluctant rebels, insisting on the limits of papal power and generally covering synodal politics with a focus on the politics—a style that implicitly conceded the possibility of the very changes that theologically they considered impossible."[72]

> Meanwhile, liberal Catholics had suddenly turned ultramontane: they were papal supremacists who found interventions like the cardinals' letter[73] impertinent, absolute believers in the Holy Spirit's tight control of doctrinal deliberation, and firm clericalists when it came to any objections raised to [the Kasper] Proposal or the synod proceedings from outside the papacy and hierarchy. . . .
>
> In defense of a populist pope who scorned "doctors of the law," liberals claimed that the Kasper Proposal's wisdom was something that only (liberal) doctors of theology could understand; in defense of a pontiff who attacked clericalism they complained about not only cardinals but conservative pundits and bloggers and tweeters rushing in where only serious Churchmen ought to tread.[74]

This last sentiment, that such considerations should have been left to higher-ups in the Church, has found an echo outside of liberal Catholic corridors. Dave Armstrong, a theological and political conservative, has said much the same: "My position is that popes should be accorded the proper respect of their office and criticized rarely, by the right people, in the right spirit, preferably in private Catholic venues, and for the right (and super-important) reasons."[75]

The end result of the synodal process, says Douthat, was something of a draw. "Relative to every prior magisterial statement on the subject [of marriage], the synod's language was ambiguous and unstable. But relative to what the pope had plainly wanted and what conservatives had feared, it was only a shift of rhetoric, not one that touch doctrinal substance."

The pope himself seemed to feel that he had been balked and outmaneuvered, judging from his closing address to the synod, which read more like an outburst than a summation, from a leader angered in defeat. Gone was the evenhanded, balancing speech of the 2014 synod. In its place came a frontal assault on the conservatives who had resisted him. He compared them to the older brother in the parable of the prodigal and the jealous laborers in the parable of the vineyard workers, and that was the kind part.

They stood accused of "a facile repetition of what is obvious or has already been said"; of "burying their heads in the sand" and repeating prohibitions in "language which is archaic or simply incomprehensible"; of using

Jesus' message as "dead stones to be hurled at others"; of sitting "in the chair of Moses and judg[ing], sometimes with superiority and superficiality, difficult cases and wounded families"; of giving in to "conspiracy theories and blinkered viewpoints"; and above all of a "fear of love" that had strangled Christian mercy.[76]

Moving on from a discussion of the two-part synod, Douthat turns to the papal exhortation that ultimately came from it, *Amoris Laetitia* ("The Joy of Love") which was issued five months after the synod closed and which was "the longest papal document in history—two hundred and fifty-six pages, some sixty thousand words."[77] (As a comparison, *To Change the Church* is a bit under eighty thousand words.)

Referring to the final document from the synod and *Amoris Laetitia*, Douthat says, "A casual reader, reading the two papal documents together, would have no doubt that Francis wasn't so much developing John Paul's thought [as in *Veritatis Splendor*] as arguing with it. . . . It was clear that chapter eight of *Amoris Laetitia* yearned in the direction of changing the Church's rules for Communion, that its logic suggested that such a change was reasonable and desirable. Yet the pope never said so directly, never made explicit what he repeatedly implied, never simply came out and said: *For many of the divorced-and-remarried, the Church's law is too hard to follow, the moral dilemmas too extreme, and therefore they cannot be considered to be seriously sinning and can receive Communion in good conscience.*"[78]

This might be the most judicious comment on the pope's actions and views, with respect to the synod and *Amoris Laetitia*, to appear in any of the books under discussion. Certainly there was a "logic" in that document's eighth chapter, but just as certainly the consequences of that logic were not stated clearly or emphatically. Parts of the document admitted of multiple interpretations, some of them more probable than others. If there was no assurance that the pope had intended to change doctrine—assuming, for the sake of argument, that he could—there equally was no assurance that he affirmed the traditional teaching regarding who might be eligible to receive Communion.

Douthat asks, "What were those 'certain cases' where the sacraments might be given? Well, the strong implication of the papal language was that they included some cases where people continued to live in public adultery. But the footnote [number 351] did not say so clearly; instead it very deliberately said so unclearly, leaving open the possibility that like prior papal documents those 'certain cases' only included people trying to live as brother and sister, trying to be chaste."

Which meant that *Amoris Laetitia* left the Church in a bizarre position. After two synods, two years of heated argument and deep division, the pope's great matter came down to a strange question: could long-standing Church discipline and a core moral teaching be rewritten via a suggestive footnote to a deliberately ambiguous papal exhortation? Not just the synods themselves but decades of debates about how far the Church could go to accommodate modernity, how much change could be allowed, were all suddenly distilled into a strange sort of textual parsing.

Depending on your interpretation, *Amoris Laetitia*'s drift proved that the pope *could* change what his recent predecessors had taught was unchanging and essential—which would be a Church-shaking, revolutionary development! Or else, just as plausibly, its lack of clarity proved that even a pope who wanted to change a major teaching was constrained—by the Holy Spirit?—from doing so. . . .

On the other hand, there were conservatives (among them Cardinal Raymond Burke) for whom those footnotes and formulations were too dangerous to be ignored and who therefore pressed the case that *Amoris* was not actually a fully magisterial document, that as a mere apostolic exhortation (as opposed to a papal encyclical) it could be corrected, challenged, or ignored.[79] . . .

Then there were those middle-grounders who wanted to accept *Amoris* in full while also acknowledging that the footnotes did point to some relaxation of the rules for the reception of Communion and who therefore labored to make that relaxation fit with prior teaching, prior doctrine. This case for continuity was made by several prominent figures linked to John Paul II and Benedict—including Rocco Buttiglione, an Italian philosopher and jurist, and Christoph Schönborn, an Austrian cardinal and theologian assigned to explain *Amoris Laetitia* to the press.[80]

But multiple readings were possible and reasonable, and because the pope had declined to choose explicitly between them, all of them were embraced, by theologians and Catholic scribblers and bishops all around the Catholic world, as the true interpretation of *Amoris*.[81]

I will leave Douthat's further consideration of *Amoris Laetitia* and its unclear interpretation. Enough, I think, has been quoted to demonstrate his evenhandedness, his fairness in looking at the document and the preceding synodal process. Now let's look briefly at his take on what happened to high-ranking clerics who did not toe the invisible but obvious line. This brings us back to a consideration of the administrative style of Pope Francis and away from matters of doctrine per se.

Meanwhile, Francis also moved to undermine and isolate the conservatives who remained in prominent Vatican positions. Letter-of-thirteen signatory Robert Sarah, the head of the Congregation for

Divine Worship, had his wings clipped after he gave a speech urging priests to celebrate Mass *ad orientem*—toward the altar, toward the east, the traditional manner abandoned after Vatican II. He was summoned to a meeting with Francis, the Vatican spokesman slapped him down publicly, and then in a remarkable purge most of his subordinates were removed and a more liberal roster of cardinals and bishops put in place—effectively leaving Sarah as a conservative figurehead with no effective power.

Other purges followed: several priests were fired from Müller's CDF for no apparent reason (the real reason seemed to be that Francis had heard through back channels that they had criticized *Amoris*), and lesser entities like the Pontifical Academy for Life found their membership rolls emptied and replaced with a new roster of papal favorites.[82]

It certainly is within papal prerogatives to hire and fire at will, but historically popes have exercised their transformational powers slowly and with respect for traditional processes. "Both John Paul II and Benedict had prodded the Vatican and the episcopate in a more conservative direction by degrees, promoting their own men while also respecting the normal processes that turned auxiliary bishops into archbishops, archbishops into cardinals. In general but especially after the synods, Francis seemed to be on a more hurried timetable."[83] Thomas

Reese, a leading American Jesuit, approved, saying that "all my progressive friends are certainly pleased with these appointments . . . But then I have to be honest with myself by asking the question, 'How would I have reacted if Pope John Paul or Pope Benedict had done the same thing?' Frankly, I would have been outraged."[84]

Over the following months it became clear that there was something of a disjunction between the controversy that was in the headlines during and immediately after the synods, up through the issuance of *Amoris Laetitia*, and the way most Catholics viewed what had gone on. Most of them, naturally enough, hadn't paid much attention to the proceedings. Few of their predecessors, generations earlier, had paid much attention to the goings on at Vatican II, which was a far more imposing and important gathering than were the recent synods. This should have surprised no one. It always has been the Catholic way, as undesirable as it might be. Most Catholics, throughout history, have been oblivious to Vatican maneuverings, even those who, especially in modern times, had ready access to information about what had been occurring.

Douthat astutely notes that the lack of interest, on the part of most Catholics, was "cited by the pope's partisans: because there was no crisis in the pews in the strange months after *Amoris*, they argued that there was no crisis whatsoever."

Just as they had suggested during the synods that any conflict was a creation of the media, in the wake of

*Amoris* and the *dubia* many of Francis's admirers argued that the division over the pope's teaching wasn't very serious, that Burke was a melodramatist and other critics attention seekers and the journalists giving them aid and comfort were desperate for a headline, that the document itself was quite clear and not remotely controversial to most Catholics, that anyone who murmured about schism or fretted about heresy was a hysteric.[85]

These sentences well describe the position of commentators such as Dave Armstrong and Pete Vere. The latter repeatedly has argued in Facebook posts that the absence of evidence of widespread discontent among everyday Catholics suggests that conservative critics of Pope Francis have gone off the reservation. "Move along, please; nothing to see here"—that seems to be the implication. Neither Vere nor Armstrong has criticized directly high-level Churchmen such as Cardinals Burke, Sarah, and Müller for giving resistance to the pope at several levels, but the two apologists have been persistent in saying that, in the long run, things come down to tempests and teapots.

So what might come from all of this, in Douthat's mind? He asks, "[C]an the Francis revolution really be resisted?" Can its opponents—and mere foot-draggers—be overcome?

To imagine a future in which it succeeds, one need only extrapolate some of the institutional patterns of his pontificate forward: his appointees continue to fill in the highest ranks within the Church and his critics age and retire and die; his approach to remarriage and Communion is accepted as a legitimate development of doctrine because after a time there are no Burkes or Sarahs to contest it; there is no rebellion in the pews because enough Catholics are either liberal or indifferent or conditioned to accept whatever the pope has handed down.

And finally conservative resisters, like similarly situated believers in certain Protestant denominations, either depart for some schismatic alternative or remain as an unhappy church-within-the Church, noisy and grumbling but sidelined and irrelevant.

So by staying alive and forging ahead, in this analysis, the man who was Jorge Bergoglio can ensure that the future of Catholicism will be progressive, liberal, *new*—whatever that may ultimately mean.[86]

Douthat doesn't claim that this is what will happen. He says this is what might happen. It is one of several scenarios, none of them impossible, none of them certain. What is certain, he says (or at least implies) throughout his book, is that this pontificate has been notable for the disarray and confusion that have welled up during it. No little blame, he thinks, has to be laid at the feet of Francis himself. "His highly personalized style, his willingness to 'make a mess' in the service of internal revolution, his insult-rich rhetoric, his impatience with circumspection, tradition, and taboo."[87]

How will things end up? It depends. Francis's successors may "sustain his revolution. If they do not, if it collapses from self-contradiction and the halfway house of *Amoris* gets demolished, he will be remembered with Boniface VIII in the ranks of ambitious popes who over-reached and with Honorius and John XXII in the ranks of popes who failed to teach and keep the Catholic Faith."[88]

> The early images of the Francis era were missionary images, an iconography of faith-infused outreach. The later images have been images of division— warring clerics, a balked and angry pope, a Church divided by regions and nationalities, a Catholic Christianity that cannot preach confidently because it cannot decide what it believes. . . .

> Francis has not just exposed conflicts; he has stoked them, encouraging sweeping ambitions among his allies and apocalyptic fears among his critics. He has not just fostered debate; he has taken sides and hurled invective in a way that has pushed friendly critics into opposition and undercut the quest for the common ground. Like Boniface after Celestine, Francis has pressed papal authority to its limits—theological this time, not temporal, but more dangerous for that.[89]

Douthat ends his book with a quotation that appears in Paul Vallely's *Pope Francis*, a 2013 biography that received wide praise. The quotation is from a Jesuit in Argentina who knew fellow Jesuit Jorge Bergoglio.

> As provincial he generated divided loyalties: some groups almost worshiped him, while others would have nothing to do with him, and he would hardly speak to them. It was an absurd situation. He is well-trained and very capable but is surrounded by this personality cult which is extremely divisive. He has an aura of spirituality which he uses to obtain power. It will be a catastrophe for the Church to have someone like him in the Apostolic See. He left the Society of Jesus in Argentina destroyed with Jesuits divided and institutions destroyed and financially broken. We have spent two decades trying to fix the chaos that the man left us.[90]

Douthat concludes: "Francis likes to say, 'Make a mess!' In that much he has succeeded."

* * *

Writing at the website of *The Federalist*, columnist Rachel Lu—a convert who teaches philosophy at the University of St. Thomas—looked at *To Change the Church* and had these observations in a review[91] of the book:

> The pews haven't refilled and the Church hierarchy is more bitterly divided than ever, displaying the kind of politicization that predictably followed Francis's

willingness to set aside normal promotional patterns, removing people he regards as troublemakers, and promoting outsiders who are more sympathetic to his views and agenda. (In a Catholic context we normally talk about "hermeneutics of continuity" rather than "illiberalism," but the problems are relevantly similar to what we're seeing in Western politics as polarizing populist leaders erode our political traditions and civic norms.) If the 2013 world was waiting for a Catholic rebirth, she is still waiting.

Once a charismatic headline-maker, Francis now exercises his influence mostly through the cudgel of administrative authority. Scandals have surfaced, and the curia has seen no noteworthy reforms. Reading Douthat's book, I suddenly wondered, "Does the Holy Father still say outrageous things on planes, or did he stop?" Maybe he still says them and we just don't care anymore. It's telling that I wasn't sure.

What happened to the beautiful dreams of Francis's salad days? The most obvious problem was that he gave the faithful too many compelling reasons to worry about his orthodoxy. Although he never formally jettisoned Catholic dogma concerning the indissolubility of marriage, the pope's aggressive push for "pastoral accommodations" for the divorced and remarried left little doubt as to his true wish. The implications of literally abandoning a millennia-old dogma are almost unthinkable. (Are we going to issue apologies to the liberal Protestants for our years of stubborn intransigence in the face of their enlightened reforms? Why would we even pretend to be Christ's Church anymore?)

Francis's actual strategy—formally retaining the teaching, but pushing hard to reduce it to dead letter—was less catastrophic than that, but it's still the ecclesial equivalent of a weak handshake. It's more or less the opposite of what one would need to inspire a burning sense of mission in the Catholic faithful.

Beyond the orthodoxy concerns, the fact remains that a "radical Catholic center" needs to stay in the center. Francis's efforts along these lines broke down severely when the sought-after unity didn't immediately emerge (and critics did). Certainly, we can have some sympathy for the Holy Father on this front. As we regularly see in the political realm, it's difficult to stand as a judicious mediator among deeply divided factions. Very few have the necessary patience, prudence, and perspective.

But those qualities are simply required if one hopes to draw a divided people back together. By surrounding himself with like-minded friends, and crankily castigating his critics as hard-hearted

Pharisees, the pontiff effectively shelved his own plan for a less factional and more mission-oriented Church. In the long run, an ability to deal charitably with detractors is more important than a willingness to pick up one's own luggage from the conclave hotel.

In these comments, Lu is sharper, more pointed, in her criticisms than are many other writers. That may in part be a consequence of her writing a book review rather than a book. In a book one is able to develop an argument at leisure, as Douthat has done. In a review, one must get right to the point, leaving unsaid things that might put events and persons into a wider perspective. Moreover, a review—or a blog post—needs to raise its voice above that of a book just to get attention.

That said, Lu largely echoes Douthat in her understanding of what Francis has done and what he seems to have intended. Like Douthat she says that Francis began his reign with a public expectation that he would make substantial reforms. Those reforms have not come, in large part, she thinks (as does Douthat) because they have been undercut by the pope's style and machinations. Conservative critics of Francis might see this as an unintended blessing. Had he favored honey over vinegar, his plans might have progressed further. In the meantime, the vinegar has tasted sour in the mouths of those at the receiving end of his chastisements or reassignments.

That seems to be Lu's take on things and Douthat's too. It is not everyone's take.

* * *

Here are excerpts from an interview of Ross Douthat that appeared at the website of *The American Conservative*[92] on March 27, 2018. The interviewer was journalist Rod Dreher, who posts there at length almost daily. Formerly a Catholic, and before that brought up as a Protestant, Dreher now is Eastern Orthodox. At the end of this section I add comments about Douthat's responses.

DREHER: What is the thesis of your book?

DOUTHAT: That Pope Francis, through complex maneuvers, is trying to liberalize Roman Catholicism's approach to morality and modern life in something like the fashion that progressive Catholics have hoped for, secular observers have expected, and conservatives have insisted is impossible ever since the Second Vatican Council. That his project, and the resistance he has met from bishops and cardinals and theologians, has pitched the Church into a theological crisis that will be remembered and studied alongside Jesuit-Jansenist debates and Arian-Athanasian battles. That the pope himself has taken a great gamble, one that is likely to make him remembered as either a genius or a near-heretic, and either way to leave the Church profoundly changed.

DREHER: Though not a Catholic, I try to follow Catholic news, because I think that as goes the Roman

Church, so goes the West. Why should non-Catholics care about your book?

DOUTHAT: [ . . . ] In particular, I think the Francis era in Catholicism will tell all Western Christians something important about the plausibility of the thesis you advance in *The Benedict Option*—that so-called "liquid modernity" will dissolve every Christian confession that doesn't hold fast to tradition. The Vatican under Francis has been critical of your argument and for understandable reasons: their vision, what you might call The Francis Option, is very different because it assumes that there are all kinds of ways that the Faith might adapt and change to suit the times and that such adaptation requires leaving the "rigidity" associated with conservatism and Traditionalism behind. And if the pope's reformation succeeds, if Catholicism adapts in the way he and his intimates envision and then thrives and evangelizes more successfully, it will supply a kind of explicit counter to your vision and a different model for Christian flourishing in our challenging cultural matrix.

If it succeeds; if it fails or leads Catholicism deeper into division, it will offer a rather different set of lessons. . . . We talk a lot about the idea of a crisis of liberalism in our political debates these days; well, the question of whether an institution like the Catholic Church can successfully liberalize without destroying its own integrity, whether it can thrive in a form more adapted to the liberal order, is very relevant to broader political and cultural questions of whether liberal society can sustain itself long term.

Then last but hardly least, everyone should care because the Church of Rome is the one true Church, so the fate of the entire human race is effectively at stake when Catholicism goes into crisis. But surely that goes without saying.

DREHER: I kept thinking as I read *To Change The Church* about how few Catholics seem to understand what's really at stake in what on the surface looks like a merely pastoral move by Pope Francis. One of your reviewers, the Cambridge scholar Richard Rex, says that the Roman Church is facing its worst crisis since the Reformation. Yet the sense of crisis seems to be limited to a relatively small number of engaged Traditionalists. What are the rest of the world's Catholics not seeing?

DOUTHAT: I think the strongest argument against my thesis is that it can't be a major crisis if there isn't tumult in the pews. There was much more chaos on the ground after Vatican II than there has been under Francis. And of course there's nothing like the dockside fistfights over the nature of Jesus' divinity that characterized Mediterranean life during some of the Christological controversies of the fourth and fifth centuries, to say nothing of the literal wars of the Reformation. . . .

So in part this crisis seems muted because he's worked to keep it that way, proceeding through ambiguous formulations and footnotes and decentralizing permission slips. The theory in his inner circle seems to be that this is the way to get Catholicism where they want it to go without a Reformation-level blowup—that you can let national churches and local bishops conduct their own experiments, with a kind of soft pressure from Rome to liberalize, and with time conservatives will become sufficiently marginalized that they will lack the effective power to protest, and they'll just have to subsist as a kind of church within the Church, anachronistic in their moralism and sacramental theology just like the Church's Latin-Mass parishes are (from a progressive perspective) anachronistic in their liturgy today.

I think this plan is too clever by half, that Anglican-style decentralization in Catholicism will ultimately encourage Anglican-style division. But it's true that at the moment the pope's determination to make changes without admitting that they're changes has left most of his conservative opponents flummoxed and thereby also limited the experience of crisis for ordinary Catholics in the pews.

DREHER: Early on, you claim that the particular neuralgic points within the Church—marriage, divorce, homosexuality, for example—are really symbols of much deeper questions and problems. Give an example of what you mean.

DOUTHAT: You can see this very easily in the crucial test case for the Francis agenda—his push to allow some or all divorced-and-remarried Catholics to receive Communion. The existing discipline, the rule that his predecessors reaffirmed, doesn't exist because of some generalized thing called "conservatism" or even "sexual conservatism." It's entirely possible to have a conservative religious perspective that allows for divorce, as Islam and Judaism both attest—and indeed a lax approach to divorce is entirely compatible with certain patriarchal norms. Rather, what conservative Catholics are trying to conserve is Jesus' radicalism, which is apparent enough in the clear words of Scripture (his disciples are not exactly pleased to hear about marriage's indissolubility) and which has been ratified and reaffirmed for centuries by Church teaching and tradition.

So the debate over divorce and remarriage, while clearly driven by the sexual revolution, cannot help but become a debate about deeper issues, about Christ and the Church. What does Scripture say, and how firmly does it bind? When can tradition change? How much do we trust the Church's interpretations of Jesus? How much do we trust the Gospels? How much do we trust Jesus himself?

DREHER: In one of the later chapters, you draw a very important distinction about the difference in the Gospels between law and mercy. Speaking of Jesus, you say that he offers mercy and forgiveness to sinners, "but he never confirms them in their sins, or makes nuanced allowances for their state of life; that sort of rhetoric is alien to the Gospels. The ritual law—yes, that can and must be superseded. But the moral law—no, that is bedrock." You go on to say that Francis challenges this paradigm, which is why his papacy is "potentially revolutionary." Would you elaborate?

DOUTHAT: Much of the reformist rhetoric of the Francis era, from the pope himself and from his allies, has drawn an analogy between the contemporary Church's conservatives and the New Testament's Pharisees—portraying the former group as exactly the kind of "doctors of the law" against whom Jesus often railed, who piled on pointless legalistic burdens instead of offering healing and mercy. This is a very rhetorically powerful argument, because these are some of the most memorable conflicts in the Gospels, and Jesus really was arrayed against the religious authorities of his day, really was radically forgiving, really was happy to hang out with publicans and prostitutes and so forth.

But the analogy doesn't actually fit with the way Jesus talked about morality; he didn't always sound precisely like a theologically-conservative Catholic, but neither did he sound at all like a certain kind of Francis-era liberal. He was a fierce critic of legalism and dead ritual, yes, but the moral law's demands—especially everything related to money and sex—he generally made more absolute, not less. And a big part of his case against the legalism of the Jewish authorities was that it effectively offered lawyerly excuses for people to evade their moral responsibilities, to qualify the Ten Commandments, to escape the clear demands of God. . . .

The bottom line is that there is no moment in the Gospels that I can see where Jesus makes the kind of situational-ethics, "sometimes the law's just impossible to follow" move that's common to liberal Catholicism these days and that you can find woven into Pope Francis's big document on marriage and the family, *Amoris Laetitia*. In the Gospels it's radical forgiveness and radical moralism all the way down, not ambiguous accompaniment and "well, it's not ideal, for now it's okay." . . .

But the debate over Communion for the remarried isn't a debate about inclusive gestures or personal accompaniment; it's a debate about whether the Church's teaching on indissolubility should be considered an essential truth or just a kind of notional ideal, a none-too-binding guideline. And I don't think you have to squint very hard at the worldly European clerics with rich and mostly-empty churches who are coming up with clever theological rationales for modifying Jesus' commandment and the Church's law in order to satisfy the demands of the post-sexual revolution bourgeoisie to see that if someone is playing the Pharisaical part in this dispute, it's not necessarily the conservatives. . . .

And in a similar way, my impression is that the most popular aspect of the Francis pontificate for a lot of young people who consider themselves "left-Catholics" of some sort isn't all the "let's make peace with the sexual revolution" business; it's this pope's more radical critiques of modern capitalism and the whole technocratic world order, which the young see—not unreasonably—as a kind of effective enemy of Christianity. Which is why you have more overlap between younger left-Catholics and younger right-Catholics—between the would-be "Tradinistas" and the would-be integralists—than you had between the neo-conservative and neo-liberal Catholics who set the terms of intra-Catholic debate after the 1960s, because for the rising generation, there's a general loss of confidence in the whole system of liberalism that manifests itself whichever end of the spectrum you swing toward.

Again, there's selection bias at work here: These kind of right-Catholics and left-Catholics are overrepresented on Catholic Twitter and among the writerly set, and there are plenty of young Catholics and young Christians who are less discontented and disillusioned, who aren't interested in esoteric debates about liberalism, and who either like Francis in much the same way they liked John Paul II (without necessarily paying close attention to intra-Church debates) or else like him for the same reasons that the secular press likes him—because he's a "cool pope" who doesn't make them feel guilty about having premarital sex or supporting same-sex marriage.

But it still seems to me that there is more genuine radicalism among Catholics younger than myself than in the recent past, and as the Church shrinks and their radicalism becomes more influential, it will have some very interesting and very unpredictable implications for the fights within the Church that I'm writing about and the way the Church relates to the secular world.

DREHER: One great strength of *To Change the Church* is its tone and its approach. It is clear where you stand, but you go out of your way to be fair to Francis, and to consider things from his point of view. And you avoid the polemical tone that has characterized a lot of Catholic writing critical of him. To me, both those choices make your argument much more effective.

DOUTHAT: That's very kind of you, but you're already sympathetic to my argument; I can direct you to quite a few reviewers who don't share your view of my fair-mindedness. The truth is that I'm somewhat less polemical because I'm less certain than some of the Holy Father's critics about the best alternative to his accommodating approach. Francis's fiercest critics are Traditionalists who have a very coherent view of what's gone wrong in the Church that folds in a number of post-1950s changes that I have long thought were either good or necessary or both; his second-fiercest critics are John Paul II conservatives who firmly believe that the JP2 synthesis was the only definitive interpretation of Vatican II and that all the Church needs to do is return to what John Paul taught.

I am not a Traditionalist, though I think that the Francis era has lent more credence to Traditionalist arguments, but nor am I convinced that the last two popes offered the last word on the Church's relationship to modernity, on what can and cannot change. I think the Church is in search of synthesis and will be for some time—all the way, perhaps, to another ecumenical council that actually settles the many questions that rushed in after Vatican II. So despite my sincere criticism of the pope, a spirit of uncertainty seems like a necessary part of that criticism, if I'm being honest about my own position and the rather confused position of the Church.

Plus, Francis is the pope and I pretty obviously am not. So my criticism has to at least try to be fair-minded, however much it might fall short, or else I am clearly failing in my duty as a member of his flock.

* * *

As Rod Dreher notes, "One great strength of *To Change the Church* is its tone and its approach." Ross Douthat avoids "the polemical tone that has characterized a lot of Catholic writing critical of him." That tone has characterized not just writing critical of the pope but writing in defense of him too. If there has been name-calling and labeling among his critics, so has there been among his defenders—not all of his critics, by any means, nor all of his defenders but enough on each side as to close, partially or completely, the opposing side's ears.

Douthat sees Pope Francis as taking a high-stakes gamble. It may or may not pay off. The result might be a new and higher synthesis, or it might be a generations-long weakening of the Church. Other critics, such as Phil Lawler and Henry Sire, are more sharp in their words (the latter considerably more than the former), perhaps because they think the stakes are higher or perhaps because they think they have a more concrete sense of how the gamble will play out.

In the meantime, things not only are in flux but they

appear to be in flux to many observers, both inside and outside the Church. One observer, who had been an outsider but recently converted to Catholicism, replied to another post that Dreher wrote about the pope. The anonymous commenter said this:

> I just converted. In a world where your phone is obsolete within a year and everything is constantly changing, it is a comfort, a dignity, and a blessing to be part of an eternal Church. Except they are trying to change it fundamentally. Between reading the news and finishing Douthat's new book, it is really depressing to see the Vatican making so many fundamental mistakes.

> I think Francis thought that if he just shook things up and stood back, God's will for a decentralized, progressive Church would unfold. It didn't, and I don't think he has seen the error. It's easy to blame resistance on a few vocal, retired Traditionalists, but the young Catholics are trending more traditional. I converted because I fell in love with Catholicism, the Eucharist, and strong moral convictions. If I wanted Episcopal, Presbyterian, or Lutheran Christianity, I had those options. I converted because I genuinely love Catholicism, and many Catholics, including the pope, seem to be somewhat ashamed of it. How do you gain converts if you asterisk half the catechism?

I realize it is a bit selfish to be late to the party and not want anything to change, but I am genuinely annoyed. Just based on what I read in the news and see in my area, the Catholic Church is suffering from a serious crisis of conviction.

So here we have someone, likely fairly young, who was looking for moorings, thought he found them, and now is wondering whether he tied his boat to an untethered buoy. He is but one example of people who admit to being confused by what has been going on in the Catholic Church during this pontificate. He, and others like him, therefore are Exhibit 1 against the claim that "no one is confused by Pope Francis." Many people claim to be confused, or puzzled, or torn within, and it seems only proper to accept their perceptions of what they are feeling and thinking. Yet some defenders of the pope repeatedly state that there is no such confusion.

To some extent, of course, there always is confusion about papal doings, and there always has been, among Catholics and non-Catholic alike. (One need not have worked four decades as a Catholic apologist to understand this.) That is not the sort of confusion that people such as the recent convert above refer to. They mean a new sort of confusion, one that comes from the top down rather than from the bottom up.

* * *

Three days before Rod Dreher's interview with Ross Douthat was published Dave Armstrong presented his take on *To Change the Church*. He wrote at his blog at Patheos under the title "Protestant Takes Solace in Douthat's Pope-Bashing Book."

"Pope bashing" is a term that Armstrong uses repeatedly. An independent observer might imagine someone using fisticuffs against the Holy Father or at least the verbal equivalent, but Armstrong applies the term to just about any sustained criticism of Francis. He hasn't applied it to people who have said that the pope ought to have answered the four cardinals' *dubia* promptly. That is a position Armstrong himself takes, and occasionally he acknowledges the pope's infelicity of expression, but anyone who goes much beyond that in criticism, whether in a book or online column, becomes a "pope basher" and engages in "pope bashing."

I find this labeling less than helpful, at two levels. It obscures distinctions or nuances. The writer who strays slightly from Armstrong's comfort zone is as much a basher as one who is about to jump into fevered sedevacantism. Terms such as "pope basher" do an injustice to most of those against whom they are employed. They also do an injustice to Armstrong himself. Such terms makes him look flustered, unable to work up an argument satisfying not just to others but even to himself: that is how most people take it when others resort to such labeling. It usually backfires on Traditionalists who repeatedly talk about the "disaster" of Francis's latest action, no matter how anodyne that action might be. If everything is a disaster, nothing is a disaster. Likewise, if every critic of a pope is a "pope basher," who except the somnolent would not be? Even Armstrong himself could qualify is the eyes of someone even more ready to employ the term—after all, he has made mild criticisms of Francis.

Armstrong begins in an ironic vein:

> It's Ross Douthat who is being used as a puppet of the devil, not Pope Francis. There are many "blessings" that flow from the current slew of best-selling pope-bashing books: Phil Lawler's *Lost Shepherd* (see my many articles on that) and Ross Douthat's *To Change the Church: Pope Francis and the Future of Catholicism*, that I specifically address now:

> 1. They help to undermine the faith of the average Catholic (whether they think logically or consistently about it or not) in Catholic ecclesiology, the institution of the papacy, infallibility, and indefectibility. Thus (mark my words) they will lead to many abandoning the Church.

Let's pause here and make a note of Armstrong's prediction. When Francis was elected, many wrote of an anticipated "Francis effect," saying that soon many would flock to the Church, now that it had a personable head who clearly had a heart for the poor and dispossessed. (Such comments were unfair to John Paul II and Benedict XVI.) But the "Francis effect" so far has not materialized. There has been no discernible influx into the Church. Will there be the opposite now that at least three books (Armstrong fails to mention Henry Sire's *The Dictator Pope*) critical of the pope are receiving considerable attention?

"[T]hey will lead to many abandoning the Church." How many is "many"? I would be surprised if there were no readers of those books who, influenced by them but not encouraged by them, fashioned a logic of their own and concluded that, with Francis, the Church has failed in its mission and needs to be abandoned for something else, but I doubt that I ever would hear of more than a handful of such people, most of whom likely would have left the Church anyway but find the brouhaha concerning Francis to be a good excuse to cut ties.

Still, it will be instructive to see to what extent Armstrong's prediction pans out, even if "many" turns out to be entirely the wrong word.

2. They undermine the traditional characteristic of reverence and deference towards the pope, as the leader of the Church, which follows scriptural injunctions concerning honor and respect towards rulers and leaders.

3. By undermining the papacy, indirectly, other Catholic doctrines also become implicated. The relatively unsophisticated Catholic in the pews (and pubs) starts to question things, because he or she hears the false rumors that even the pope has done so.

If pews and pubs are filled with unsophisticated Catholics who now start to question things, it isn't likely that any of them will have heard, let alone read, any of the three books. Their lack of sophistication suggests that whatever they learn comes from the secular media—large parts of which, for instance, claimed that the pope had denied the existence of hell, a confusing and erroneous assertion. It seems that Armstrong is not pointing to the real culprits.

4. They make a laughingstock out of the Catholic Church, since even non-Catholics know that the pope (and his office) ought not be treated with such contempt; and it is a disgraceful, utterly unseemly outward display to the watching world. As such, it works against people seriously considering becoming Catholics.

No one reading the three books fairly—and this is particularly true of Douthat's—could say that the authors treat Pope Francis with contempt. Sire's book is the most tendentious; he offers up a few claims for which he gives no substantiation at all, but even then he doesn't write contemptuously of the pope or of his office. Armstrong has gone full dudgeon without reason—and without justice to the three writers.

5. And it confirms Protestants and Orthodox in their mistaken views that the papacy is unbiblical and a

non-necessary office in the first place. The first thing Martin Luther did when he decided to go his own way and revolt against the Catholic Church was attack the pope. And he did so with lies, talk of the "Antichrist," and scurrilous, mocking illustrations. This approach remains a key trait of anti-Catholic rhetoric, lies, and polemics to this day. The last thing I did before yielding up my own strong Evangelical Protestantism and bowing to the wisdom of the ages in the Catholic Church was fight ferociously against papal infallibility, as I have written about in great detail. . . .

The devil's victory today is that he has Catholics inside the Church doing the work traditionally reserved for non-Catholic critics (i.e., they are "useful idiots"). He just sits back and enjoys himself, watching the stupidity and gullibility of Catholics and laughing and mocking us to scorn. Now we have the pathetic spectacle of millions of Catholics en masse, judging and lying about the pope, gossiping about him and trashing him on a regular basis. . . .

Above, Armstrong predicted that criticisms by the three authors "will lead to many abandoning the Church." Here he claims that "millions of Catholics" are "judging and lying about the pope." This is quite a leap. I wonder whether it is even the case that "millions of Catholics" are talking about the pope at all, whether pro or con. Most

Catholics probably get through the week not giving the pope the least thought. If controversy about him catches their attention one minute, it is gone from their attention the next.

I suppose there will be some who will stop considering the claims of the Catholic Church once they see a pope is not above criticism; they will have imagined him to have been imbued, at his election, with knowledge or capabilities he did not have when a lowly cardinal. Such people, when they enter the Church—and this has been true for at least the last two centuries, ever since ultramontanism became something of a modern force—eventually discover that every pope brings into the Vatican the disabilities and character he had before the conclave. The result often enough has been that such starry-eyed converts become disillusioned and return to their former allegiances.

As for Protestants and Orthodox, they all along have disagreed about papal prerogatives, authority, and power, so it is not easy to see how internal Catholic disputes would harden them against a papacy they already reject or hold suspicions about.

Douthat said that "Francis is not a theological liberal." He was mostly critiquing his economic and social views (it's the typical regrettable either/or dichotomy between the Church's doctrinal and social teaching), and contending that he was too lax against the liberals in the Church.

Douthat lacked faith in the indefectibility of the Church already by then, and he bashed Vatican II, which is the second of the three hallmarks of the radical reactionary Catholic (the other two being pope-bashing and Ordinary Form/Pauline Mass-bashing). Thus, the stage was set for his current no-holds-barred attack against the pope. He wrote:

"Conservative Catholics need to come to terms with certain essential failures of Vatican II. For two generations now, conservatives in the Church have felt a need to rescue the real council, the orthodox council, from what Pope Benedict called 'the council of the media.' . . . The council as experienced by most Catholics was the 'council of the media,' the 'spirit of Vatican II' council, and the faithful's experience of a council and its aftermath is a large part of its historical reality, no matter how much we might wish it to be otherwise. But its deliberations simply took place too soon to address the problems that broke across Catholicism and Christianity with the sexual revolution and that still preoccupy us now. Which is not to say that what the Church needs right now is a Council of Trent, exactly. The recent synod on the family suggests that, if attempted, the outcome would be either empty or disastrous."

In other words, Douthat is thinking like a reactionary in two of three key respects. That's the backdrop of his papal bashing now. I replied to this paragraph in my paper about him:

"What has occurred is no more the failure of the council itself than it is a failure of Pope Francis when the media and popular secular culture distort his view on a given subject. This is not an essential failure of Vatican II. Douthat seems particularly confused on this point: throwing out the baby with the bathwater. The misguided liberal 'spirit of Vatican II' only proves that people delude themselves about the magisterium and try to spin and distort it to the public. The fault for that lies on those who do it, not the council. Is this not utterly obvious?"

If one were to see only this characterization of *To Change the Church*—as a "no-holds-barred attack against the pope"—a reading of the book might be a great disappointment, because it wouldn't live up to Armstrong's characterization. It might be said legitimately that Louie Verrecchio has entered upon a "no-holds-barred attack against the pope." With somewhat less justification one might say that also of Christopher Ferrara of *The Remnant*. But Douthat's writing is probably the least tendentious, the most conciliatory, the most gentle of all the prominent but Francis-critical writing out there today.

For Armstrong to say that Douthat engages in a "no-holds-barred attack against the pope" seems like an act of petulance on his part. He repeatedly complains that papal critics fail to give Francis his due, but has he given them theirs?

Douthat says that "conservative Catholics need to come to terms with certain essential failures of Vatican II," but Armstrong says that the things Douthat complains about do not constitute "an essential failure of Vatican II." Armstrong insists there were no essential failures; Douthat insists there were. This may appear to be a contradiction, but I think the two are saying—please pardon the expression—essentially the same thing, but they are using "essential" in different ways.

Armstrong uses it in a Thomistic sense, as referring to the inner nature of a thing: to say that an ecumenical council has "essential failures" means that it fails even to be an ecumenical council, which is a council specially guided against error by the Holy Spirit. Douthat uses the term in a colloquial, non-philosophical way: Vatican II had "essential failures" in that things that flowed from it—or, more precisely, flowed after it but not necessarily because of it—failed to live up to expectations portrayed in the media even while the council was in session. Pope John XXIII famously wanted to open windows to let the light in, but with the light came the smog of modern incredulity and venality.

Next Armstrong returns to his *bête noire*, the author of *Lost Shepherd*.

I've documented how Phil Lawler was also starting to attack Vatican II itself. . . . Lawler—just like

Douthat—questioned the authority of an ecumenical council (Vatican II). He did this in an article at his Catholic Culture site, dated 23 August 2017:

"Did the problems that arose after Vatican II come solely because the Council's teachings were ignored or improperly applied? Or were there difficulties with the documents themselves? Were there enough ambiguities in the Council's teaching to create confusion? If so, were the ambiguities intentional—the result of compromises by the Council fathers? . . . The proponents of change can cite specific passages from Council documents in support of their plans. So are those passages being misinterpreted? Are they taken out of context? Or are there troublesome elements of the Council's teaching, with which we should now grapple honestly? One thing is certain: we will not solve the problem by pretending that it does not exist."

This is classic reactionary thinking, folks. I know that, because I have studied the reactionary mindset closely for over twenty years. I have a major web page devoted to it (probably the most extensive from any orthodox Catholic) and have written not just one but two books on the topic.

I'm doing my job as a Catholic apologist: studying serious errors within the Catholic milieu and warning people about them, showing how and why they are wrong. This sort of lack-of-faith, gossipy, fear-mongering mentality lies behind the current pope-bashing. The chain of thought, from one error to another, is clear as day. . . .

"This is classic reactionary thinking," says Armstrong. But what he quotes from Lawler is indistinguishable from classic conservative thinking too. For half a century conservative writers have pointed to sections of the conciliar documents—particularly pastoral sections—that can admit of more than one emphasis or even of more than one interpretation. This is hardly surprising because pastoral provisions, almost by their nature, are fluid. The same matters, written about by a council that would have convened fifty years earlier or later would have been handled in somewhat different ways, as reflective of the Church and society of those times.

Lawler asks whether the language of Vatican II was sufficiently open that proponents of doctrinal change could make a *prima facie* case for their positions. That seems to be a fair question. Provisions of earlier, more tightly-written councils were misconstrued, sometimes unintentionally, sometimes with bad intentions. Have some teachings of Vatican II been "taken out of context?" asks Lawler, repeating a question that orthodox Catholic have been asking for two generations—generally with the implication that the proper answer is "Yes."

Armstrong calls this "classic reactionary thinking," but

it would seem to be "classic conservative thinking" if anything. His stereotypic reactionary would not so much ask whether the council's documents have been misconstrued; instead, he would argue that the documents contained outright errors, something that those who have engaged in "classic conservative thinking" have not done.

Then back to Douthat.

> It's clearly Douthat who is thinking like a Protestant and a Catholic reactionary (notorious for thinking like Protestants). After all, he is deliberately undercutting, questioning, bashing the authority of both a pope and an ecumenical council: both things that Protestants characteristically (and at least self-consistently) do. Luther attacked the pope and he attacked councils as self-contradictory (they "can and do err": so said he at the Diet of Worms in 1521) [and] therefore untrustworthy.

> Douthat and Lawler precisely parrot Luther, dissident Catholics, and reactionary Catholics. And that's why their books (not even getting to their innumerable errors and fallacies) are so outrageous and spiritually (even morally) dangerous to the flock and to non-Catholics as well. Avoid them—and the gossip and trash-talk that invariably surrounds them, in com-boxes and cocktail parties—like the plague, and warn others to do so as well.

So, in the end, Dave Armstrong sees Phil Lawler and Ross Douthat (and, no doubt, the unmentioned Henry Sire) as imitators of Martin Luther and, simultaneously, as mimicking left-wing Catholic dissidents and right-wing Catholic reactionaries. The authors, however mild or spirited their criticisms of the pope, however well established their facts, are "dangerous to the flock" and must be avoided, and others must be warned against them.

As I mentioned earlier, Armstrong is a long-time friend of mine. He is orthodox in his beliefs and has worked effectively as a Catholic apologist for many years. He prides himself, with no little justification, on his precision when it comes to defending Catholic teachings and history. Often he finds himself at odds with anti-Catholic writers, whether Protestant or unbelieving, and with the more heated exponents of the Catholic Traditionalist position. He has complained about opponents not giving him a fair shake, of taking his words out of context, of presuming he says things that he doesn't say. Understandably, he has shown frustration at his opponents' misreading of his positions. (One becomes tired of swatting away the same flies.)

I am unable to explain why he fails to give to papal critics the courtesy and consideration he faults others for not giving him.

# Chapter 4

# Nothing So Salutary

There are four national Catholic weekly newspapers in the United States: *National Catholic Reporter*, *Our Sunday Visitor*, *National Catholic Register*, and *The Wanderer*. These are listed from left to right: from liberal (and often heterodox), to mainstream or moderate, to conservative, to more conservative. Historically, the staff of *The Wanderer* has shown little reluctance to criticize (liberal) bishops and priests but much reluctance to criticize popes, except in anodyne terms. That has changed with the current pontificate.

An article in the January 25, 2018 issue is indicative of the new approach. Editor Joseph Matt wrote under the headline "*Amoris Laetitia* and the Pope's Deafening Silence."[93] The adjective immediately signaled that this would not be a litany of praise. Matt summed up his position in the opening line: "Countless petitions, open letters, heartfelt editorials, endless pleas from concerned Catholics, bishops, and cardinals, filial corrections, and even a plea in the form of *dubia* have all resulted in a deafening silence from the Holy Father."

The next line is tough language for *The Wanderer*, at least for language about a pope: "Pope Francis through his failure to clarify or his unwillingness to acknowledge that there is a serious issue with the infamous chapter 8 of *Amoris Laetitia* implies a complicit approval if not an advancement of the dissident thought that is surrounding this harmful document."

Before we move on, let's parse this sentence. It has several notes to it. Francis is accused of a "failure to clarify." This wording is blunt but fair, since in fact the pope hasn't clarified chapter 8. He is accused of harboring an "unwillingness to acknowledge that there is a serious issue" with that chapter. Again, that's correct, though it presumes that there is an issue, serious or otherwise, with chapter 8. If there isn't an issue at all, or if the issue isn't serious, then this complaint would be misplaced.

Next, chapter 8 of *Amoris Laetitia* is labeled "infamous." This is an unfortunate term, one that can be found in much controversial writing, whether of the left of right, whether about religion or politics. Something disapproved of is called "infamous," more or less heedless of whether it really has risen to the level of infamy. For Americans, the word usually brings to mind Franklin D. Roosevelt's December 8, 1941, address to Congress, in which he referred to the previous day as "a date which will live in infamy." "Infamy" seemed apt in that situation, but, by comparison, "infamous" seems overblown when referring to an exhortation the chief controversy of which resides chiefly in a footnote.

"Infamous" is what rhetorician Richard M. Weaver called a "devil term": it has little content of its own; its purpose is to express disapproval. Something slapped with the label "infamous" at once becomes less worthy of consideration, less respectable. It implicitly is rejected by right-thinking people. Weaver said, "A singular truth about these [devil] terms is that, unlike several which were examined in our favorable list [what Weaver called "god terms"], they defy any real analysis. That is to say, one cannot explain how they generate their peculiar force of repudiation. One only recognizes them as publicly-agreed-upon devil terms."[94]

Few things, no matter how bad, ever rise to the level of true infamy, but many people throw around the word "infamous" to categorize something they don't like. Just as something can't be famous unless it is widely known, so it can't be infamous unless it is widely known. The attack on Pearl Harbor was universally known within hours or days. Chapter 8 of *Amoris Laetitia* remains unknown even to most educated Catholics two years after its release. It hardly, with justification, could be labeled either famous or infamous.

Last—still in the second paragraph of his article—Matt calls *Amoris Laetitia* a "harmful document." How is that to be taken? Is the whole exhortation harmful—or just chapter 8? Is the whole of chapter 8 harmful—or just a few sentences or footnotes? Is the harm sufficiently isolated that it is unfair to leave the impression that the whole document is harmful, or is the harm such that, like a malignant yeast, it affects (or infects) the whole of the dough?

In his third paragraph Matt uses a word that is not as tendentious as those in the previous paragraph. He calls *Amoris Laetitia* a "troublesome document." That seems a fair descriptor, if a troublesome document is one that has engendered trouble, and *Amoris Laetitia* surely has. Proof of that is the controversy surrounding its interpretation and, as corollaries, the variant interpretations given to parts of it, such as chapter 8, in various parts of the world.

Matt then lists "practical consequences" that flow from the troublesome nature of the exhortation. Evangelization (especially convert making) will suffer if the Church appears as wavering in its teaching as have the multitudinous denominations that split off from Catholic unity. Catechizing will suffer as parents find difficulty in conveying the faith to their children, who "are extremely adept at picking up moral shortcuts and seeing through false and phony arguments." Priests will suffer in that they will be confronted with couples about to be married who think they have been given leeway that didn't exist before.

To use Lenin's question, "What is to be done?" Matt says, "As laypeople, we grow weary with frustration because we are limited in how we can resist this assault on our Church [referring here not to Pope Francis but to heterodox Catholics and others who use the exhortation for their own ends]. We must live out our faith to its fullest on a daily basis and insist to our clergy that the teachings of Christ cannot be tampered with. And, of course, we cannot discount the power of prayers, through which we can be of enormous help regarding this current crisis.

"Ultimately it will be the magisterium of the Church that will have to remedy this situation, and that is where we can plead with our bishops and cardinals to take action on this issue. As the crisis in the Church escalates, the time is now for a formal declaration to be issued on the key areas of Church doctrine that are 'not clear' in Pope Francis's teachings by the magisterium of the Church."

Matt goes on to endorse a "formal correction for the good of the Church"—that is, a correction of the pope by cardinals and bishops, who also belong to the magisterium. "We are running out of time," he says. "Each passing day will bring this crisis to a worse level." He recommends that Pope Francis resolve the problem "with the simple removal of chapter 8 from *Amoris Laetitia*." Here he quotes Fr. Gerald Murray, from the latter's appearance on EWTN's *The World Over* on January 11, 2018: "Indeed, my hope and prayer is that *Amoris Laetitia* chapter 8 would be withdrawn, because I think it's causing huge problems in the life of the Church."

"The pope can be criticized on any number of grounds," concludes Matt, "but it is hard to deny that chapter 8 of *Amoris Laetitia*, by all logical accounts, is an attempt to change doctrine. There is no other way to look at it. As Catholics we pledge obedience to our pope, but when our pope conflicts with the teachings of Christ we must take issue with that, and it appears to even the casual observer that on this issue of chapter 8 of *Amoris Laetitia* the pope is wearing no clothes."

Until his last paragraph, Matt doesn't offer much

criticism to the person of the pope. The criticism is directed to a document from the pope—or, more precisely, to a single chapter within that document. Fair enough. He draws near his finale by saying, "The pope can be criticized on any number of grounds." I take this as meaning that he can be criticized on matters other than this one exhortation. Fair enough again, and true enough. The comes a twofer: we owe obedience to a pope, but we can criticize a pope (does this constitute disobedience in Matt's mind?) if the pope teaches something contrary to the teachings of Christ.

Here, as I mention elsewhere in this book, is a conflating of distinct things: obedience and agreement regarding interpretation or teaching. It is not obedience to a pope to consent to his teachings. A pope doesn't order Catholics to consent. He may order them to refrain from discussing something, and in that case obedience would enter the picture, but to consent to a papal teaching is—or at least should be—to *assent* to the truth within that teaching. If it happens that a pope teaches (informally, say) something certainly false, such as that the Old Testament has 39 books rather than 46, then a Catholic is free not to assent to that teaching, and in doing so he is not being disobedient because obedience simply isn't relevant to the matter at hand.

We come finally to Matt's last—and rather unfortunate—words: "the pope is wearing no clothes." There are two things wrong with this formulation. First, it's trite. Journalism of all sorts, whether religious or secular, would be better off if it never made allusion to that emperor of fable. Second, Matt's words here are ungenerous and ungentlemanly. In the fable, only the emperor thinks he is wearing clothes. All his retainers and all the onlookers realize he isn't. In the case of Pope Francis, it hardly is the case that only he thinks that chapter 8 of *Amoris Laetitia* is without problems. Many of his defenders think likewise, be they heterodox or orthodox in their general persuasions.

Thus Joseph Matt ends his article with something of a thud. *The Wanderer* might be termed a traditional but not a Traditionalist publication. No long-time reader should be surprised at its finding fault with *Amoris Laetitia* or even, on occasion, with the pope. Throughout its century-and-a-half existence *The Wanderer* has been a consistent defender not only of the papacy as an institution but also, without exception, of the popes who have reigned during that time. Francis is the first pope against whom the publication has voiced substantial criticism. Sometimes that criticism is a bit arch.

* * *

A gentler criticism can be found in the writings of Dwight Longenecker, who grew up Evangelical, attended Bob Jones University and then Oxford University, and became an Anglican priest. He converted to Catholicism, became a Catholic priest, and serves a parish in South Carolina. He is a popular writer, apologist, and speaker. He wrote a blog post titled "How Should Someone Criticize the Pope?"[95] In it he gave his own sense of what should (and should not) be done.

There has been some feedback from readers who were disturbed by a recent post of mine encouraging folks not to fret too much about the pope and to continue to get busy at the local level doing what they can with what they have where they are. I still think this is the best advice for the majority of the faithful.

What worries me about a lot of the online criticism of the pope is that much of it seems based on mainstream media headlines, the breathless articles from extreme right-wing websites, the harsh criticism from alarmist bloggers and social media pundits. Furthermore, too often the criticism is uninformed or only partially knowledgeable and written by folks who have too often jumped to conclusions and are blinded by their own prejudices and personal likes and dislikes.

However, does that mean I think we should put our head in the sand and pretend all is happy in the garden? Not at all. We are not called to be either Catholic robots or Catholic Pollyannas. Where criticism is needed, the right people, whose calling and charism it is, should speak out, but they should do so in a powerful and proper way.

This week at The Catholic Thing[96] and Crisis[97] there are two articles which illustrate what I think is a proper kind of critique of the present state of affairs in the Catholic Church. The first article is by a priest, Fr. Jerry J. Pokorsky. Here's why it's a good article:

1. Fr. Pokorsky avoids personal attacks on the pope. There's no name calling or calling the pope "Bergoglio."

2. It is not emotionally charged. The article isn't a breathless diatribe against the pope.

3. It is informed and balanced. Fr. Pokorsky gives good reasons for his critique.

4. It does not come across as self-righteous, rigid, or holier than thou.

5. The tone is not complaining, whining, or petty.

6. It focuses on the larger issues, not just on specific nit-picky problems.

7. It helps us understand the smaller problems as symptoms of a deeper and wider malaise in the Catholic Church.

8. It returns us to the priorities of the Faith: our soul's salvation and the reverent worship of God.

9. It offers a positive attitude in the midst of worrying details.

This is the sort of intelligent, wise, and measured critique that is needed because it highlights the faults of our current situation in the Catholic Church and calls for the right, good, and positive response. In other words, Fr. Pokorsky's article does not just criticize Pope Francis. It does not point out what is wrong as much as what is lacking, and when we see what is lacking we can begin to fill in what is missing, and that is a positive and good thing, which grumbling and carping rarely accomplish.

Fr. Pokorsky . . . [lauds] the triumphant proclamation of the Christian gospel by Pope St. John Paul II (which had history-changing implications); he contrasts this with Pope Francis:

"Under the current pontificate, that bold Christian triumphalism has given way to a kind of stealth secular triumphalism—with calls for dialogue, open immigration, and environmentalism—rarely an invocation of Jesus. During his recent 'Address to Authorities, La Moneda Palace' in Chile, Pope Francis complimented the Chileans on their beautiful country and advances in democracy. He urged them to avoid consumerism and to address environmental problems. But the Holy Father continued a pattern he established in America during his speeches to civil authorities. He carefully avoided mentioning 'Jesus,' 'Lord,' and 'God.' As a result and perhaps by intention, he appeared primarily as a visiting head of state, with a mostly secular policy agenda."

The second article is by the inimitable Fr. George Rutler at Crisis. Entitled "Where Are the Churchmen with Chests?", in it he speaks about the present spinelessness of our leadership but puts it in a larger historical context. As Fr. Pokorsky criticizes the pope for preaching a secular gospel in Chile, so Fr. Rutler points out the same defect in Pope Francis's address to Congress in the U.S.:

"A pope is not merely another head of state, and the whole history of the economy of Christ and Caesar makes clear that popes are never stronger than when they are weakest in things temporal. Surely a man resolved as Pope Francis is to do what is right for mankind was ill-served by those who counseled him on what to say in addressing a joint session of Congress. On that awkward day, the Holy Father spoke of refugees, human rights, the death penalty, natural resources, disarmament, and distribution of wealth, but there was no mention of Jesus Christ. The speech invoked acceptable figures like Abraham Lincoln, Martin Luther King, Dorothy Day, and Thomas Merton, but no canonized saint that the nation's legacy boasts."

These articles get down to the real matter at hand: the preaching of a secular gospel rather than a sacred gospel. Why have so many Catholic leaders substituted the saving gospel of Jesus Christ for a message of worldly salvation?

In this blog post Longenecker gives his take on what proper criticism of a pope looks like. As examples he mentions parallel incidents in which Pope Francis came across less as a religious leader than as a secular leader, and Longenecker—through Pokorsky and Rutler—faults him for that. He lays out, by reference to Pokorsky's comments, the attributes of proper, respectful criticism, starting with an absence of name-calling and ending with three points that uplift the faith of the reader or listener.

For all the care Longenecker takes in delineating what constitutes a legitimate criticism of a pope, it will not be enough for some people, for whom any criticism is too much.

* * *

Let me follow Longenecker's remarks with selections from an article written at the *First Things* website under the title "When Catholics Criticize the Pope."[98] This piece appeared in March 2018, before the true identity of Marcantonio Colonna was revealed. The writer was Dan Hitchens, deputy editor of the *Catholic Herald.*

C. S. Lewis never read the newspapers. Though this habit led to some memorable blunders—he was under the impression that the Yugoslav dictator Tito was King of Greece—he felt it was intellectually and spiritually healthy. If something important happens, Lewis believed, somebody will always tell you.

Some Catholics take a similar view of Church politics: it should, they say, be treated as a distant irrelevance. Frequent the sacraments, say your prayers, do your duties at work and home, feed the hungry, visit the sick; don't waste time in fruitless anxiety about what Cardinal X said to Monsignor Y about Bishop Z's remarks on the latest papal press conference. Even if you are concerned, you shouldn't go around shouting about it—that's against the spirit of obedience we owe to our superiors. And what impression does it give to the world when Catholics are at each other's throats in a Church that is supposed to be defined by unity and fraternal love?

There is a lot of truth in that. But it is not the whole truth, and now is the time to ask where its limits are, since criticism of Pope Francis is growing: three unfavorable books, by Philip Lawler, Ross Douthat, and the soon-to-be-unmasked "Marcantonio Colonna," have been or will be published in the next two months. These authors will be told that it would be better to keep silence. I am less certain.

Let's concede, for the sake of argument, that parish life goes on largely independent of actual bureaucratic decisions in Rome. Even so, the Vatican's reach, its "soft power," is incomparable. Quotations from the pope fill the official literature of dioceses and parishes, the classroom materials of Catholic schools. When millions of young Catholics gather, the pope is, humanly speaking, the main event. For the secular media—which is harder to ignore now than in C. S. Lewis's day—the papacy practically is the Church. The pope and his advisors have an unparalleled ability to decide, from day to day, what is seen as important or fashionable.

So even if one tries to ignore it, Vatican politics still works its influence. When Jean Vanier, the founder of L'Arche, shocked his admirers by expressing qualified support for assisted suicide laws, he explained: "Pope Francis continues to tell us that everything cannot be regulated by a law and there are always exceptions." Vanier's is not the only interpretation of Pope Francis's ideas—the pope is ambiguous on the question of moral absolutes. The point is that Vanier, in so many other ways a hero of the faith, might not have made such a serious mistake without the influence of the Vatican.

Vanier is just one example of how the pope changes people's minds. And if he is changing them—even by accident—in the direction of doctrinal errors, then those errors should be named and rejected. Even if the pope does not intend the present doctrinal confusion, it still calls for an urgent remedy.

Leo XIII was speaking out of a well-established tradition when he quoted an ancient warning: "There can be nothing more dangerous than those heretics who admit nearly the whole cycle of doctrine and yet by one word, as with a drop of poison, infect the real and simple faith taught by our Lord and handed down by apostolic tradition." If a single false word is so fatal, then how can Catholics ever be relaxed about major ambiguities being broadcast and major errors being allowed to spread? It is right to be on one's guard against false doctrine, and it may be right to put others on their guard too.

Some will agree with this, but say that only the errors should be pointed out, without naming names. It is not for lay people to identify false or confusing teaching from bishops, they say, let alone from popes. Which, again, is a reasonable argument. And yet, deliberately to ignore the source of an error makes that error harder to uproot. Nor is there any clear principle that says the little people in the Church cannot speak up to the great, or St. Catherine of Siena would have been wrong to rebuke the pope, and St. Thomas Aquinas and canon law would not identify a possible duty for the faithful to address their superiors "even publicly."

This is not to justify every word of mockery, anger, and vindictiveness in the Church. But the line between prideful rebellion and justified remonstration is not easily drawn. Also unclear is the question of scandal, of whether Catholics should debate these matters publicly. True, the Church is less attractive to non-Catholics when it resembles an especially vitriolic debating society. But it is also less attractive when truth is marginalized.

I have heard more often of people drifting from their faith, or being deterred from entering the Church, because of unchecked heresy than because of public disagreement. There is potential scandal in open debate—but also in pretending that everything is fine, thus making Catholicism seem a game in which one conceals one's opinion when the most serious truths are at stake.

The question of how far a Catholic can criticize a pope is at least as old as Jacopone da Todi, who wrote fierce satires on Pope Boniface VIII—while, on other occasions, abasing himself before the pope's authority and enduring excommunication in humble obedience. Although he has often been called Blessed Jacopone, the Catholic Encyclopedia tells us that he has never been officially declared saintly by the Church, probably because of those same attacks on a sitting pope.

Jacopone had less excuse, I think, than many of Pope Francis's critics; his concerns were more political than doctrinal. But his never-resolved story confirms that we do not quite know how far a Catholic may go in openly criticizing the Vicar of Christ. It remains one of the gravest questions of this strange crisis. What it calls for, to use a much-misunderstood term, is discernment.

Hitchens' take on the possibility of scandal is perceptive. Scandal, in the proper sense of throwing one off the right path, can work both ways. Will some shy away from embracing the Catholic Church because they see squabbling? Likely so, but that number should not stand in isolation, which is where many defenders of Pope Francis leave it. It needs to be compared to another number, that one resulting from people shying away from a Church that seems too enfeebled to maintain its patrimony.

I have yet to come across anyone who, considering whether to become Catholic, has decided not to take the step because he has learned that Catholics not only disagree with one another but sometimes even with the leadership of their Church, at least on procedural matters. On the other hand, I have come across many who have not taken the step because they fear the Catholic Church is going the same way as mainline Protestant churches have gone, except with a delay of a few decades. They see little reason to get on a local train that will take them to the same undesired destination as the express train.

\* \* \*

Here's the tail-end of a long comment I made on a thread started by Dave Armstrong. My comment was a response to a comment made by Pete Vere. His was in reference to discussions that had been going on for a few weeks among conservative Catholics regarding the propriety and accuracy of criticisms of Pope Francis, particularly as given in, and in light of, the three books that have been the chief focus of this book, Henry Sire's *The Dictator Pope*, Phil Lawler's *Lost Shepherd*, and Ross Douthat's *To Change the Church*, which was published the day I wrote my comment. The discussion picks up in mid-stream.

> I find the whole process fascinating: how conservative Catholics—taking that term in a wide sense—are squabbling about this pope: people whose own orthodoxy rarely can be questioned but who take such disparate approaches that they could be imagined, by outside observers, to belong to quite different dispensations.
>
> To me the interesting thing here is Rhetoric. I capitalize the term to indicate that I mean the art or science of rhetoric, as taught and practiced by the

ancients and even into our own era—or at least into my era, since I'm older than you [Dave and Pete] and true rhetoric, as a discipline and art, seems to have gone into eclipse in my youth or even my childhood. (One of the last practitioners and theoreticians of rhetoric in the U.S. was Richard Weaver, author most famously of *Ideas Have Consequences*.)

Nowadays the word "rhetoric" carries almost exclusively a negative connotation. Rhetoric is what our opponents use when unconvincingly speaking (usually insincerely) against our positions, whether political, religious, cultural, or whatever. But in truth rhetoric—which, as I emphasize, is an art—is the art of persuasion. It concerns how we get people to understand, accept, and internalized what we think to be true or right or useful.

Given human nature and the way the human mind and heart work, syllogisms often aren't enough to bring acceptance and conviction. You might think they would be—they would be to a computer, I suppose—but in practice they often aren't. They need to be bolstered by other forms of proof. (See Newman's *Grammar of Assent* for an extended argument on this.) Syllogisms are nicely clean-cut: premise 1, premise 2, conclusion. People with degrees in math, such as myself, like them. But, as I said, they often just don't work to convince people.

Consider the five Aquinate proofs. Each, taken on its own, in lofty isolation, is enough to prove God's existence, but I never have heard of anyone who moved from atheism to belief precisely because of those proofs. The five serve not so much as inducements to belief but as after-the-fact confirmations of a decision already arrived at through other means. Their syllogistic nature, for most people, just isn't enough to carry the day. Thus enters rhetoric, in basic philosophy and in other areas, such as the one we've been embroiled in for some time now.

As I said, I find the exchanges fascinating, though I don't mean by that that I've found them particularly satisfying intellectually. I think there's been more dross than fine metal. I hope to have more to say in about the rhetorical aspect of these ongoing discussions. For me it will be amusing, but I hope also useful, to see what I can make of a situation which I try to observe as a third-hand observer while also being a first-hand participant.

And thus I end where I began, as both an insider and outsider, as someone trying to be objective while taking a subjective part in discussions.

I hardly expect this book to settle anything. The issues addressed here will play themselves out during the remainder of the current pontificate and in the years following. It is likely that the greatest fears of the pope's critics and defenders will not come to pass. In retrospect the claims that Francis has been one of the worst popes in history—perhaps even at or near the top of that unsavory list—will be seen as overblown. So too, though, will the claims that he ought to be remembered as Francis the Great. Most people, particularly most Catholics, when looking back at the Francis papacy will see strengths and weaknesses, not only in the reign in general but in the man himself. A few people will persist in seeing only strengths or only weaknesses, but that will be a reflection more of their private needs than of public actuality.

It is less easy to predict what shape conservative Catholicism will be in a decade or so after Francis leaves the scene. Will heated words have been forgotten, strained friendships repaired? Will resilience have returned to the movement? Or will there be fractures that admit no healing, fissures that keep factions further apart than in the days of Benedict XVI and John Paul II, when there were tensions enough among conservative Catholics?

Most of the people I have quoted in these pages I know. Some I know well and have worked with over the course of years. Others I know through the occasional email or meeting. Still others I know only through their writings. I don't doubt the sincerity of any of them, though some of them I think to be sincerely wrong on some points. Nearly always I can agree with their motives, even if I feel it necessary to rebut their arguments. These are not people who wish ill for the Church, the pope, or the Catholic faithful, and I suspect that each of them would concur that the disputes illustrated in these pages demonstrate not just the factuality of the Fall but the necessity of the Church, the one being unbearable without the other.

Sometimes we remember quotations imperfectly. One slightly-misremembered quotation that has stuck in my mind for years comes from Pope Leo XIII's 1891 encyclical *Rerum Novarum*, the first of the social encyclicals. I prefer the way I recall his words to what he actually wrote, but I don't think that pontiff would object to my reconstruction, which goes like this: "There is nothing so salutary as to view the world as it really is." I have produced a corollary: "There is nothing so salutary as to view ourselves as we really are," a sentiment that confessors and spiritual directors likely agree with.

In these pages I have tried to show the general form of pope-related disputes that conservative Catholics have been engaged in during the last few months. I hope I have been able to show the disputes "as they really are," giving a just picture of each of the parties. By necessity I have had to leave out more than I have been able to include. Readers— and the people mentioned in these pages—may wonder why I omitted *this* topic or *that* exchange. My excuse must be lack of space, time, and endurance. A truly full examination of these disputes would require a book several times the length of this one, and even that book would be incomplete. Besides, I have another writing project, longer than this one, to turn to, so I must call a halt to this one.

I wish I were like the college president in Randall

Jarrell's novel *Pictures from an Institution*, a fellow who, when asked how he could get so much done, replied that "there are thirty-two hours in every day, if only you know where to look for them." I have yet to discover those extra hours. I fear I never will. They could be employed usefully in trying to take the measure of the current pontificate and the controversies concerning it.

# Thank You!

I hope you found this book useful or informative—preferably both! If you did, please consider leaving an honest review at Amazon. Two or three sentences would suffice. It is through reviews that writers find most of their new readers.

If you would like to learn more about my books—those already available and those in the works—please visit my website, KarlKeating.com, where you can join my mailing list, take advantage of discounts, and be among the first to learn about new releases.

# Other Books by Karl Keating

**Debating Catholicism**

In lively public encounters Catholic apologist Karl Keating goes head to head against prominent anti-Catholics:

Peter S. Ruckman, a chief proponent of the King James Only position and a foe of all things Catholic;

Jim Blackburn, an adult convert to Catholicism who became a virulent anti-Catholic preacher and riled a whole town;

José Ventilacion, a minister in the Filipino Church of Christ, which teaches that Christ was not divine, the Trinity is a hoax, and the early Church apostatized;

Bartholomew F. Brewer, a former Catholic priest who spent years drawing Catholics out of the religion of their upbringing.

Included in this omnibus volume are four complete books:

*The Bible Battle*
*High Desert Showdown*
*Tracking Down the True Church*
*Face Off with an Ex-Priest*

These exchanges cover a wide range of anti-Catholic charges—doctrinal, historical, and scriptural. Does the anti-Catholic side have the better argument—or no argument at all? Does the Catholic response win—or does it wilt? No matter what your own beliefs may be, you'll find these debates engaging, provocative, and even amusing.

## Apologetics the English Way

Can a reasonable case be made for Catholicism? Maybe even a compelling case? Or does the Catholic argument falter? Does it fall before critiques from top-notch opponents? Judge for yourself. You don't have to be Catholic or even religious to relish the intellectual sparring that goes on in these pages.

Here is high-level controversial writing, culled from Karl Keating's favorite books. Each selection is a forceful exposition of Catholic truth. Most are from the 1930s, all come from English Catholics, and all are aimed at a single antagonist, with the public invited to look over the writer's shoulder. The reader can view the weaknesses and occasional mistakes even of his own champion.

These pages are filled with vivid personalities. These were men who knew the Catholic faith and could explain it to others. The individuals against whom they wrote may not have been converted—one or two were, in the long run—but any number of readers of these little-known masterpieces must have found their faith bolstered and their doubts assuaged. The issues covered in these exchanges are still discussed today—but probably nowhere in as glorious a style as here.

## The New Geocentrists

Were Copernicus, Galileo, and Kepler wrong? Does Earth orbit the Sun, or does the Sun orbit Earth? For centuries, everyone thought the science was settled, but today the accepted cosmology is being challenged by writers, speakers, and movie producers who insist that science took a wrong turn in the seventeenth century. These new geocentrists claim not only that Earth is the center of our planetary system but that Earth is motionless at the very center of the universe.

They insist they have the science to back up their claims, which they buttress with evidence from the Bible and Church documents. But do they have a case? How solid is their reasoning, and how trustworthy are they as interpreters of science and theology?

*The New Geocentrists* examines the backgrounds, personalities, and arguments of the people involved in what they believe is a revolutionary movement, one that will overthrow the existing cosmological order and, as a consequence, change everyone's perception of the status of mankind.

## No Apology

Karl Keating has been a Catholic apologist for nearly four decades. In these pages he shares some of his own experiences and some stories from times past.

He writes about how to do apologetics and how not to. He defends the very idea of apologetics against a theologian who thinks apologetics is passé. He looks at how the Faith is promoted through beauty and through suffering. He takes you from his own backyard to such distant times and places as fifth-century Jerusalem and sixteenth-century Japan.

## Anti-Catholic Junk Food

You are what you eat. That is as true of the mind as of the body. Eat enough greasy food, and your silhouette will betray your culinary preferences. Give credence to enough greasy ideas, and your mind will be as flabby as your waistline.

This book looks at eight examples of religious junk food, things that have come across Karl Keating's desk during his career as a Catholic apologist. You likely will find these morsels unconvincing and unpalatable, as you should. The problem is that plenty of people—including people on your block—consider such stuff to be intellectual high cuisine.

### Jeremiah's Lament

For many, the best way to reach an understanding of the Catholic Church is to see how other people misunderstand it. This book is full of misunderstandings.

The people quoted in these pages came to their

confusions in various ways. Sometimes it was by reading the wrong books or by failing to read the right books. Sometimes it was a matter of heredity, with prejudices passed down from father to son and from mother to daughter. At other times errors were imbibed at the foot of the pulpit, in the university lecture hail, or from door-to-door missionaries.

Whatever their origin, misunderstandings are misunderstandings. They should be recognized for what they are and set aside, even if that means a break from personal habit or family tradition. That is true particularly of the Church that Christ established because to misunderstand her is to misunderstand him.

How to Fail at Hiking Mt. Whitney

Often, the best way to succeed at something is to learn how to fail at it—and then to avoid the things that lead to failure. There are books that tell you how to succeed at hiking Mt. Whitney. This book helps you *not* to fail by showing you what *not* to do, from the moment you start planning your trip to the moment you reach the summit.

You learn what gear not to buy and not to take, how to maximize your chances of getting a hiking permit (don't apply for the wrong days of the week!), how to prepare yourself physically without over-preparing, how to avoid being laid low by altitude or weather problems, how not to take too much food or water—or too little. You even discover how to shave a mile off the trip by using little-known shortcuts that can make the difference between reaching the summit and reaching exhaustion.

Most people who depart the Mt. Whitney trailhead fail to reach the top. Some fail because of things entirely beyond their control, but many fail because of insufficient preparation, false expectations, and basic errors of judgment. Their mistakes can come at the beginning (such as failing to get a hiking permit), during the preparation stage (such as being induced to buy "bombproof" gear), or during the hike (such as not heeding bodily warning signs).

Through engaging stories of his own and others' failures, Karl Keating shows you how to fail—and therefore how to succeed—at hiking the tallest peak in the 48 contiguous states.

# About Karl Keating

Karl Keating holds advanced degrees in theology and law (University of San Diego) plus an honorary doctor of laws degree (Ave Maria University). He founded Catholic Answers, the English-speaking world's largest lay-run Catholic apologetics organization. His best-known books are *Catholicism and Fundamentalism* (nearly a quarter-million paperback copies sold) and *What Catholics Really Believe* (about half that many sold). His avocations include hiking, studying languages, and playing the baroque mandolino. He lives in San Diego. You can follow him at his author website and on Facebook:

http://www.KarlKeating.com
http://www.facebook.com/KarlKeatingBooks

# Notes

1 https://www.amazon.com/Dictator-Pope-Inside-Francis-Papacy-ebook/dp/B079GPBV17/ref=tmm_kin_swatch_0?_encoding=UTF8 &qid=1525319863&sr=8-1. In this book I refer to the ebook version, which was the only one available at the time of writing. A somewhat revised printed edition was published in late April 2018.

2 Philip F. Lawler, *Lost Shepherd* (Washington, D.C.: Regnery, 2018).

3 Ross Douthat, *To Change the Church* (New York: Simon & Schuster, 2018).

4 http://www.catholicworldreport.com/2017/12/13/the-dictator-pope-is-sometimes-frustrating-but-filled-with-valuable-insights-and-information/

5 http://www.catholicworldreport.com/2017/12/13/the-dictator-pope-is-sometimes-frustrating-but-filled-with-valuable-insights-and-information/

6 http://www.catholicworldreport.com/2017/12/31/the-best-books-i-read-in-2017/#james-kalb

7 https://www.thecatholicthing.org/2017/12/06/the-dictator-pope/

8 https://www.thecatholicthing.org/2008/06/02/the-catholic-thing/

[9] https://en.wikipedia.org/wiki/Robert_Royal

[10] https://onepeterfive.com/about/

[11] https://onepeterfive.com/the-dictator-pope-mysterious-new-book-looks-behind-the-mask-of-francis/

[12] https://www.lifesitenews.com/news/the-dictator-pope-reveals-francis-as-downright-vindictive-catholic-commenta

[13] Jason Morgan, "Francis is Using the Communists, Not the Other Way Around," *The Remnant* (April 17, 2018) https://remnantnewspaper.com/web/index.php/articles/item/3853-francis-is-using-the-communists-not-the-other-way-around

[14] https://akacatholic.com/about/

[15] https://akacatholic.com/poison/

[16] G. K. Chesterton, *Orthodoxy* (London: John Lane, 1909), 30.

[17] Ibid., 31.

[18] https://akacatholic.com/on-francis-and-sedevacantism/

[19] https://akacatholic.com/the-latest-stunt-from-the-bergoglian-circus/

[20] https://akacatholic.com/message-to-roman-curia-big-humble-is-watching/

[21] https://akacatholic.com/is-bergoglio-under-the-control-of-satan/

[22] https://www.trafficestimate.com/akacatholic.com, accessed 1/23/18.

[23] https://www.trafficestimate.com/lifesitenews.com, accessed 1/23/18.

[24] https://www.amazon.com/Lost-Shepherd-Francis-Misleading-Flock/dp/1621577228/ref=asap_bc?ie=UTF8

[25] https://www.catholicculture.org/about/leadership/bio_phil_lawler.cfm

[26] https://www.catholicculture.org/

[27] https://www.amazon.com/Faithful-Departed-Collapse-Bostons-Catholic/dp/1594033749/ref=la_B001JP9OKW_1_2?s=books&ie=UTF8&qid=1524586557&sr=1-2

[28] Philip F. Lawler, *Lost Shepherd* (Washington, D.C.: Regnery Gateway, 2018), vii-viii.

[29] Ibid., x.

[30] Ibid., xi.

[31] Ibid., 153.

[32] Ibid., 154.

[33] Ibid., 157-158.

[34] Ibid., 163.

[35] Ibid., 190.

[36] Ibid., 191.

[37] Ibid., 196.

[38] http://www.patheos.com/blogs/davearmstrong/

[39] https://www.facebook.com/keating.karl, December 23, 2017, "Make a Note to Get This Book on Pope Francis."

40 http://www.patheos.com/blogs/davearmstrong/2017/12/quasi-defectibility-phil-lawler-vs-pope-francis.html

41 Dave Armstrong, *Pope Francis Explained*, https://www.amazon.com/Pope-Francis-Explained-Catholic-Tradition/dp/1304831604/ref=sr_1_14?ie=UTF8&qid=1524673803 &sr=8-14&keywords=dave+armstrong

42 https://onepeterfive.com/

43 http://akacatholic.com/

44 https://rorate-caeli.blogspot.com/

45 https://remnantnewspaper.com/web/index.php/articles/item/3857-pope-francis-a-pelagian-lutheran

46 http://www.patheos.com/blogs/davearmstrong/2018/01/lawler-vs-pope-francis-1-critique-of-introduction.html

47 http://www.patheos.com/blogs/davearmstrong/2018/01/lawler-vs-pope-francis-2-homosexuality-judging.html

48 http://www.patheos.com/blogs/davearmstrong/2018/01/lawler-vs-pope-francis-3-the-pope-annihilated-hell.html

49 http://www.patheos.com/blogs/davearmstrong/2018/01/lawler-vs-pope-francis-4-communion-buenos-aires-letter.html

50 http://www.patheos.com/blogs/davearmstrong/2018/01/lawler-vs-pope-francis-5-jerusalem-council-vs-ideology.html

51 http://www.patheos.com/blogs/davearmstrong/2017/12/rebuking-popes-catholic-obedience-popes.html

52 John Henry Newman, *Letters and Diaries*, Charles Stephen Dessain,

ed. (London: Oxford University Press, 1961-1972), vol. 20, 545.

[53] Letter to Lady Simeon, 10 November 1867.

[54] *Humani Generis*, 20.

[55] *Lumen Gentium*, 25.

[56] www.patheos.com/blogs/davearmstrong/2017/12/rebuking-popes-catholic-obedience-popes.htm

[57]

https://www.facebook.com/dave.armstrong.798/posts/1832310340137276?comment_id=1832774633424180&notif_id=1517065615355922&notif_t=feedback_reaction_generic&ref=notif

[58] Ross Douthat, *To Change the Church* (New York: Simon & Schuster, 2018), 1.

[59] Ibid, 19.

[60] Ibid., 164.

[61] http://www.libertylawsite.org/2018/04/24/pope-francis-mess-ross-douthat-catholic-church-to-change-the-church/

[62] Douthat, xvi.

[63] Ibid., xvii.

[64] Ibid., 74.

[65] Ibid., 74-75.

[66] Ibid., 86.

[67] Ibid., 100.

[68] Ibid., 101.

[69] Ibid., 103.

[70] Ibid., 111-112.

[71] Ibid., 112.

[72] Ibid., 120-121.

[73] A letter from thirteen cardinals delivered to Pope Francis in late 2014.

[74] Ibid., 121.

[75] http://www.patheos.com/blogs/davearmstrong/2017/12/rebuking-popes-catholic-obedience-popes.html

[76] Douthat, 124.

[77] Ibid., 129.

[78] Ibid., 130-131. Italics in original.

[79] Ibid., 132.

[80] Ibid., 133.

[81] Ibid., 135

[82] Ibid., 139

[83] Ibid.

[84] Ibid., 140.

[85] Ibid., 147-148.

[86] Ibid., 190.

[87] Ibid., 200.

[88] Ibid., 205.

[89] Ibid., 206-207.

[90] Paul Vallely, *Pope Francis* (London: Bloomsbury, 2013), 129.

[91] http://thefederalist.com/2018/03/30/pope-francis-and-the-struggle-to-seize-the-radical-catholic-center/

[92] http://www.theamericanconservative.com/dreher/pope-francis-change-the-church-ross-douthat

[93] Joseph Matt, "*Amoris Laetitia* and the Pope's Deafening Silence," *The Wanderer*, vol. 151, no. 4 (Jan. 25, 2018), 1A.

[94] Richard M. Weaver, *The Ethics of Rhetoric* (Chicago: Regnery, 1953), 223.

[95] https://dwightlongenecker.com/how-should-someone-criticize-the-pope/

[96] https://www.thecatholicthing.org/2018/01/24/of-popes-bishops-and-the-bridge-too-far/

[97] https://www.crisismagazine.com/2018/an-uncertain-sound

[98] https://www.firstthings.com/web-exclusives/2018/03/when-catholics-criticize-the-pope

Made in the USA
Middletown, DE
14 July 2020